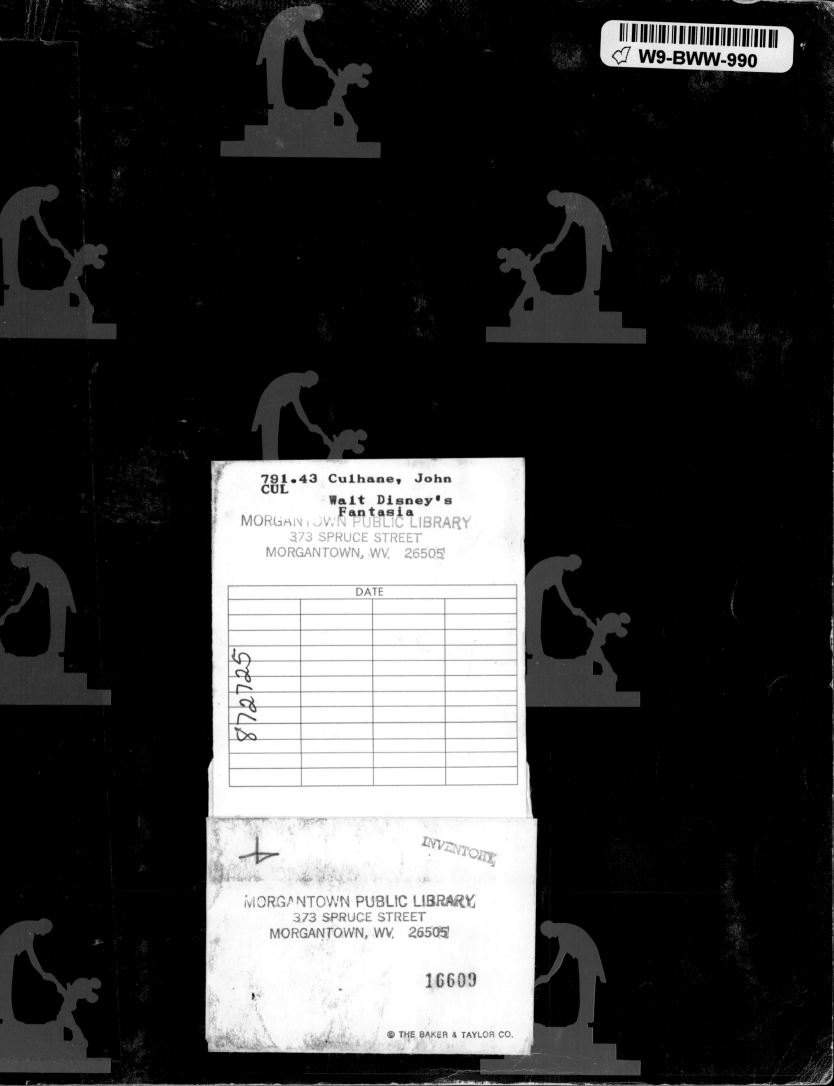

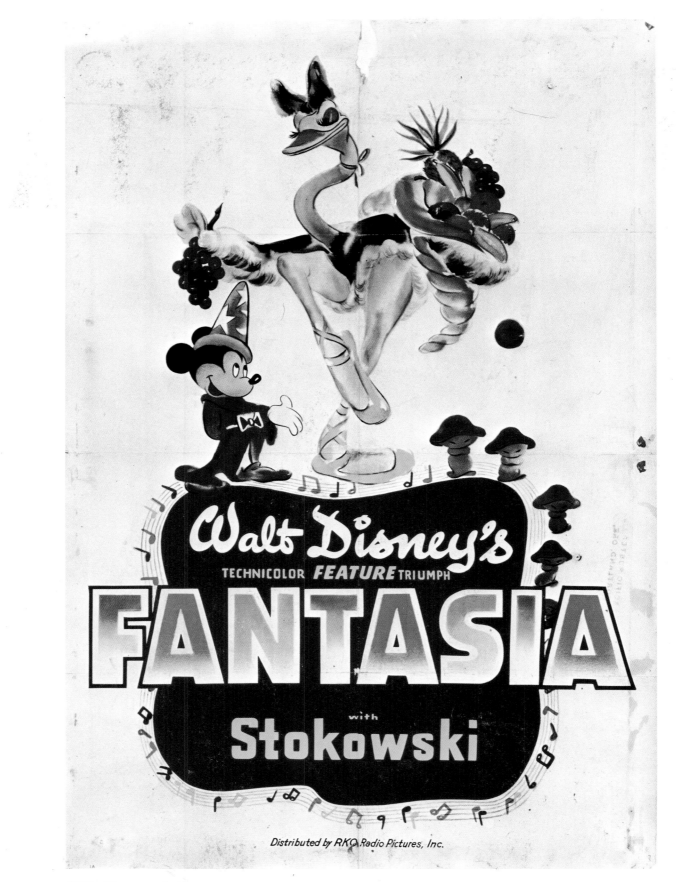

1940   The original release

# WALT DISNEY'S FANTASIA

## BY JOHN CULHANE

HARRY N. ABRAMS, INC., PUBLISHERS, NEW YORK

For
my mother and father, Isabel and Jack,
who took me to *Fantasia* with Fantasound;
and my wife, Hind, and our sons, Michael and T.H.,
whom I took to *Fantasia* with digital stereo;
and to my art teacher, Corinne Brown,
who gave me an original cel of the milkweed ballet

J.C.

Editor: Darlene Geis
Designer: Samuel N. Antupit

*Library of Congress Cataloging in Publication Data*

Culhane, John.
    Walt Disney's Fantasia.

    1. Fantasia (Motion picture).  I. Walt Disney
Productions.  II. Title.
PN1997.F3317C8  1983    791.43′72    82-24303
ISBN 0-8109-0822-0

*Printed and bound in Japan*

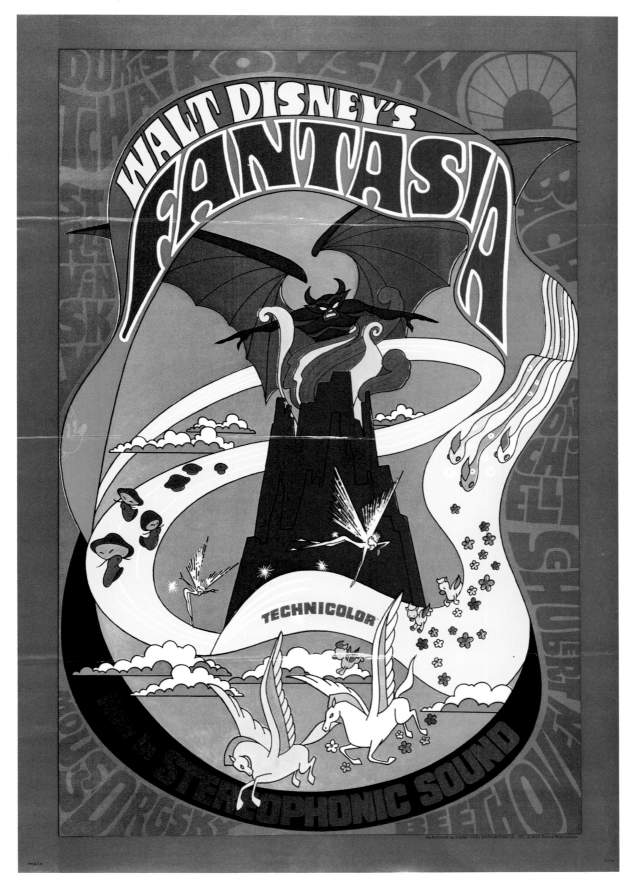

*1969   The psychedelic sixties release*

1982   *The digital release*

Fantasia *comes on the screen with an Art Deco title flash that reflects the period in which it was made.*

# FANTASIA

In a profession that has been an unending voyage of discovery in the realms of color, sound, and motion," wrote Walt Disney, "*Fantasia* represents our most exciting adventure. At last, we have found a way to use in our medium the great music of all times and the flood of new ideas which it inspires."

This Walt's-eye view of *Fantasia* appeared in the program for the film's world premiere, on November 13, 1940, at the Broadway Theater in New York—the theater that was called the Colony when Mickey Mouse made his debut there in *Steamboat Willie,* the first sound-on-film cartoon short, only a dozen years before. The statement was characteristic of the way Walt Disney's mind worked. The Tom Sawyer in Walt, hungry for respectability, insisted with his third word that the making of animated cartoons was a profession. He had vowed, when he was snubbed as a mere "cartoon-maker" seventeen years before, that his animated productions would someday be treated to the same kind of gala premieres accorded live-action films. But the Huck Finn in his personality chafed at wearing a tuxedo, and tended to see his "professional" life as an "exciting adventure," an "unending voyage of discovery" down some mythic Mississippi of the imagination.

This book on the making of *Fantasia* accompanies Walt Disney on that voyage of discovery, permitting us to watch his creative processes at work. Its principal source material has been the hundreds of pages of stenographic notes from *Fantasia* story meetings, where Disney himself took the lead.

From the beginning, Disney films were made by the story conference method. Walt—he insisted on being called by his first name—would bring together about a dozen artists and musicians in one room to play with ideas until they suggested other ideas, hopefully better, simpler, clearer, more entertaining ideas.

Everybody in the room could keep track of this play of ideas in sequence, because the ideas weren't just talked about, they were drawn as story sketches and pinned to storyboards. Storyboards were fiber boards, four feet by eight, on which the story sketches were fastened with pushpins, in rows that could be read from left to right. The sketches were made large enough so that each participant in the story meeting could see them clearly from his chair. Disney himself hadn't made a drawing since the twenties, but, in the words of Great Britain's political cartoonist and caricaturist, Sir David Low, his "was the direction, the constant aiming after improvement in the new expression, the tackling of its problems in an ascending scale and seemingly with aspirations over and above mere commercial success."

And the way Walt directed, at his best, was simply to stand up in front of a storyboard and act out the way he thought the action and dialogue should go.

For his early features, such as *Fantasia*, Disney had a stenographer present at each story meeting to record in shorthand what each participant said; these minutes — with any profanity removed — were typed, mimeographed, and circulated to those involved before the next meeting. That way each person could remember what Walt wanted, and could start figuring out ways to give it to him.

On December 8, 1938, for example, while discussing *Fantasia*'s visual complement to Igor Stravinsky's *Rite of Spring*, Walt suddenly exclaimed: "It'll be — boy! You'll really go through space!" He was talking about starting the segment with the camera in outer space, and then showing the audience what it would look like to travel from outer space to earth. And this was a quarter of a century before any astronaut had left and then reentered the earth's atmosphere. "I think it would be a terrific idea," he said, "that idea of endless space."

And, as the film so brilliantly demonstrates, his artists found a way to put that "terrific idea" on the screen for him.

To better understand the dynamics of those meetings, I have interviewed or studied interviews with scores of collaborators who watched Walt operate. "Innocence in action" is the way one of them described him. From their accounts, it is not surprising that Walt got on so well with his principal collaborator on *Fantasia*, the crowd-pleasing conductor of the Philadelphia Orchestra, Leopold Stokowski. They both had an abiding faith in the ability of the average person to appreciate the good, the true, and the beautiful.

"In my business, we'd say it another way," explained Disney. "We say that the public — that is, the audience — would always recognize and appreciate quality. It was this faith in the discrimination of the average person that led us to make such a radically different type of entertainment as *Fantasia*. We simply figured that if ordinary folk like ourselves could find entertainment in these visualizations of so-called classical music, so would the average audience."

Walt's original dreams for *Fantasia* were aimed at capturing an audience of millions for a musical film. He wanted it to be seen on a wide screen and heard with dimensional sound, so that in *The Sorcerer's Apprentice*, for example, when the brooms escape Mickey's control and march to the fountain with their water buckets, the sound would surround the audience, and the shadows of the marching brooms would reach the sides of the theater. He considered showing the abstract sequence to Bach's *Toccata and Fugue* in 3-D, providing cardboard Polaroid glasses with the program. He even discussed wafting flower scents through the audience as he presented a flower ballet to *The Nutcracker Suite*.

Disney wanted the theaters to showcase *Fantasia* as they had showcased *Gone with the Wind*, with reserved seats and matinee and evening performances, so that word of mouth could gradually build the movie's reputation as a new and revolutionary kind of film entertainment. RKO, Disney's distributor, had little enthusiasm for Walt's daringly innovative plans. They readily relaxed their contract with him and let Disney set up his own distribution unit headed by a young film salesman named Irving Ludwig. Ludwig, who was later to found Disney's own distribution company, Buena Vista, engaged prestige theaters in major cities, installed dimensional sound systems at thirty thousand dollars a unit, put in special lighting and curtain controls to set off each sequence in the film, and hired and trained the theater staffs so that audiences would be treated with the courtesy later to be associated with Disneyland.

So Disney *did* present the first stereophonic sound in *Fantasia,* calling it Fantasound; but stereoscopic cinema, aromatic cinema, and the cameras and projectors for the double-width frames needed for a wide screen were experiments that were too expensive for him in 1940.

When *Fantasia* did not immediately prove popular with the mass audience, the bankers brought pressure on Disney to cut it from 130 minutes (with intermission) to 81 minutes, and RKO took it from two shows a day and put it in general distribution on a double bill with a Western. Marketed that way, it produced a loss for Walt Disney Productions.

*Fantasia* was reissued once, in 1946, restored to its original length, and still did not recoup its original investment. "But I don't regret making it," Walt said in 1951. "It's what we should have been doing with our medium at that time."

In 1956 Disney reissued *Fantasia* a second time. And suddenly this sixteen-year-old film was appreciated by the millions for whom it was made. *Fantasia* has now been reissued numerous times, and has been in continuous release—always playing somewhere in the world—since 1969. It is among the two hundred highest-grossing films of all time. But even when it represented a financial loss to Walt Disney, after two releases and more than ten years, he spoke of it with enthusiasm in his voice and eyes. So it is easy to understand how he inspired his artists to make it in the first place.

Stokowski wrote: "I enjoyed working with Walt because of his boundless imagination and simple direct approach to everything. He had the ability to find and attract highly talented designers in form and color. His instinct for perceiving great gifts in young artists reminded me of Diaghilev."

It was an apt comparison. Serge Diaghilev, founder of the Ballet Russe, integrated the ideals of other art forms—music, painting, drama—with those of the dance to fulfill his ideal of the combination or interpenetration of the arts. Walt Disney, founder of the Walt Disney Studio, combined the ideals of music, painting, drama, and dance with those of film to create an entirely new form of film art, so that Erwin Panofsky, the distinguished art critic and historian, would write in his seminal essay, *Style and Medium in the Motion Pictures*: "Within their self-imposed limitations, the earlier Disney films, and certain sequences in the later ones, represent, as it were, a chemically pure distillation of cinematic possibilities."

By the time they began their collaboration on *Fantasia,* Disney was thirty-six, a slim, dark-haired intense man with a film star's thin mustache and eloquent eyebrows; Stokowski was fifty-six, tall, imperious-looking, and crowned with a halo of white hair that caught spotlights wonderfully—and both men were old hands at realizing

*Albert Hurter was a Swiss-born artist who, in the words of master animators Frank Thomas and Ollie Johnston, "could find a face and a personality in everything around him." Walt used Hurter not as an animator, but as an inspirational story sketch artist. When Walt began to plan his Concert Feature, he had Hurter do these inspirational sketches for the Greek mythology sequence.*

possibilities. Since making the first sound-on-film cartoon in 1928, Disney had produced the first three-strip Technicolor film of any kind, *Flowers and Trees* (1932), and played so adeptly with images that changed shape and size and color to music that historian Lewis Jacobs, in *The Rise of the American Film* (1939), called him "the first of the sight-sound-color film virtuosos." But beyond that, he was recognized around the world as possibly the greatest fantasist since Hans Christian Andersen. He had just released *Snow White and the Seven Dwarfs,* the first feature-length cartoon ever made, and during most of the time that *Fantasia* was in production, *Snow White* was earning box-office revenues that would make it the highest-grossing film in history. (It would take second place to *Gone with the Wind* in 1940.) There were only two filmmakers in those days who were always described as geniuses, without argument: Chaplin and Disney—and Chaplin was having difficulty with the transition to sound.

Sound was Stokowski's playground. "He took over a provincial orchestra in Philadelphia in 1912," wrote Harold C. Schonberg, former chief music critic of the *New York Times.* "Soon he made it the greatest virtuoso orchestra in America and, most likely, the world." Through his concerts, his recordings, and his films—and his widely publicized romance with the preeminent screen goddess, Greta Garbo—Stokowski had become, by 1938, perhaps the best-known symphonic conductor of all time.

The flamboyant Stokowski was an adventurer in sound as the down-to-earth Disney was an adventurer in film. The *New York Times* called Stokowski an "audio prophet," and his biographer, Abram Chasins, wrote that "whether we're listening to an FM radio or an LP recording or a stereophonic soundtrack of a film, we must never forget how big a role Stokowski played in its effectuation." *Fantasia* was the medium through which Stokowski made his greatest contribution to sound-on-film—which was just what Disney had wanted.

Disney's natural self-confidence was greatly reinforced by the phenomenal success of *Snow White.* The average theater admission in 1938 was twenty-three cents, and most children were admitted for a dime, yet Disney's $1.5 million feature grossed $8.5 million around the world in its first release. With the profits he began building the new, superbly equipped, $3 million Studio in Burbank, into which he and his staff moved over the period from August, 1939, until the spring of 1940, and where *Fantasia* was completed the following November. He wanted to do things with the animated film that had never been done before, and he was sure that with *Snow White*'s profits, his new studio, and a staff that had mushroomed from eight hundred in 1937 to more than a thousand while *Fantasia* was in production, he would do them. "*Fantasia* was made at a time when we had the feeling that we had to open the doors here," Disney answered, when he was asked why he made the film. "This medium was something we felt a responsibility for, and we just felt that we could go beyond the comic strip, that we could do some very exciting, entertaining, and beautiful things with music and pictures and color."

Indeed, before *Fantasia,* the most usual thing for the animated film to be compared to was the comic strip. And it is true that the taproots of the early animated films were such comic strips as Winsor McCay's *Little Nemo,* George Herriman's *Krazy Kat,* and Bud Fisher's *Mutt and Jeff.* Comic strip graphics were crossbred with the broad, visual comedy of the slapstick film shorts, those of Charlie Chaplin particularly, and the result, broadly speaking, was the animated film before Disney.

Disney upgraded form and content until, after *Fantasia,* Sir David Low would write, "In *Fantasia* he lifts the art of drawing movement right out of the 'comic' and essays for the first time serious studies of a higher plane. *Walpurgis Night (Night on Bald Mountain)* and the prehistoric sequences *(Rite of Spring)* drive right to the foothills of the New Art of the Future."

It is not true, as Deems Taylor wrote of the origin of *Fantasia* in his 1940 book on the film (a canard that has had wide circulation), that "it all began as a search for a starring vehicle for Mickey Mouse." Disney never said that; and Ben Sharpsteen, *Fantasia*'s production supervisor and Disney's close collaborator from 1929, has flatly denied the oft-reported story that, as Sharpsteen put it, "*The Sorcerer's Apprentice* was made to . . . upgrade Mickey Mouse as a character. There was no such thing."

Essentially, *The Sorcerer's Apprentice* sprang from Disney's desire to go beyond the usual animated cartoon with its combination of comic strip graphics and slapstick comedy. And the most important combination in *Fantasia* was the wedding of film graphics to classical music. Indeed, the most important factor carrying the animated film beyond its roots in comic strips and slapstick film shorts was music.

"Music has always played a very important part since sound came into the cartoon," said Walt. And, indeed, he had created the Silly Symphonies in 1929 precisely to let music take precedence over action in some of his cartoons.

Whereas in the Mickey Mouse films it was the job of the composer and/or musical director to fit the music to the action, in the Sillys, it was up to the directors and animators to fit the action to the musical score. Most often these were original scores by studio musicians; but sometimes the scores included snatches of popular songs or concert music. In fact a few bars of *Dance of the Hours,* one of the selections in *Fantasia,* can be heard in a 1929 cartoon called *Springtime.* But Walt had been trying to figure out a way to use what he called "the great music of all times," because "for my medium, it opens up unlimited possibilities."

Ben Sharpsteen, in spelling out what those possibilities were, recalled that the general public, the audience at which Walt Disney always aimed, was not so comfortable in the late 1930s with music written for the concert hall. "*The Sorcerer's Apprentice* was— to use a term—highbrow music," said Sharpsteen. "Considering it was highbrow music, it was in the reach of the public. . . . There was talk about using Dopey in it—but no, Walt didn't like the idea of taking somebody from *Snow White,* and so Mickey Mouse was, when you come right down to it . . . a good choice."

*Walt Disney crouches in front of a storyboard for*
*The Sorcerer's Apprentice and acts out the sequence*
*of drawings for Deems Taylor, who wrote and delivered*
*the narrative introduction, and Leopold Stokowski,*
*who conducted the Dukas score.*

Disney's Story Department started planning a *Sorcerer's Apprentice* short using a recording by another eminent twentieth-century conductor, Arturo Toscanini. Toscanini had conducted a military band in Italy during World War I, and in 1935 he had so loved Mickey Mouse's burlesque of a bandmaster in *The Band Concert* that he prevailed upon the manager of the theater in which he saw the cartoon to stop the show and run the short again.

Leopold Stokowski, too, had gone on record as being an admirer of the art of Walt Disney—and it was Stokowski whom Disney now met in a chance encounter.

Various versions have been given of how the unlikely collaboration of Disney and Stokowski came about, though none are from Disney himself. But in a letter that Stokowski wrote in 1967, the conductor said that it resulted from a chance encounter, and not at a Hollywood party, as has frequently been written.

"I first met Walt Disney in a restaurant," Stokowski recalled. "I was alone having dinner at a table near him and he called across to me, 'Why don't we sit together?' Then he began to tell me that he was interested in Dukas's *The Sorcerer's Apprentice* as a possible short, and did I like the music. I said I liked it very much and would be happy to cooperate with him."

Disney, of course, would have been well aware of Leopold Stokowski. Though not a great concertgoer before he started making *Fantasia,* Walt was a great moviegoer. The year before, he had seen *The Big Broadcast of 1937,* in which Stokowski conducted Bach's *Fugue in G Minor,* and in this year of 1937, Stokowski was in the hit musical *100 Men and a Girl,* with the popular young coloratura soprano film star Deanna Durbin. Stokowski played himself and conducted the "100 men" of his orchestra accompanying Miss Durbin. Durbin had already auditioned to be the voice of Snow White, but Walt found her voice "too mature." Stokowski's film with Deanna Durbin was among the most popular of 1937. "Stokowski knew the visual value of the conductor, for the audience as well as the players," wrote Yehudi Menuhin. "For the first half of the century, Stokowski epitomized for most Americans what the symphony conductor should look like, how he should behave, and in large measure he helped to popularize the symphony orchestra in North America." Walt Disney was always well aware of whatever—or whomever—the mass audience liked.

"Ah, what a scurrying there was to hide the Toscanini record we had been working with when it became known that Stokowski was due to arrive," recalled Jim Algar, whom Walt had chosen to direct *The Sorcerer's Apprentice.*

On November 15, 1937, the Story Department sent all Disney employees a special notice: "We are preparing a special short subject in collaboration with Leopold Stokowski, who will conduct his renowned symphony orchestra, 100 men strong, in his own interpretation of the world-famous descriptive score of *The Sorcerer's Apprentice.*"

The importance that Walt attached to this project can be seen in the interoffice communication of November 16 to all those

*Leopold Stokowski poses with his caricature by a Disney artist (above). Looking at Stokowski's hair while watching him record the* Fantasia *sound track, Walt whispered to Dick Huemer: "He looks like Harpo Marx." Another Disney caricaturist saw Stokowski (opposite, below) as "Stokisaurus," a dinosaur whose double tail resembled the conductor's claw-hammer coat. But Disney and Stokowski took each other quite seriously as artists. A formal portrait of the maestro is autographed "For Walt Disney, Leopold Stokowski" (opposite, above).*

who were asked for story suggestions—which, as usual, included everybody from the people actually working in the Story Department to Alois, the Swiss gardener. (The *Atlantic Monthly* reported in "Walt Disney: Genius at Work" that Alois paid particular attention to the petunias under the Story Department window so that he could hear what stories were being considered—and won several of the five-dollar bonuses that Walt frequently offered for good story ideas. Unfortunately, the *Atlantic* did not report what the gardener's ideas were, but the anecdote was a good example of the ways Walt got his whole studio involved in his productions.)

"*The Sorcerer's Apprentice* will be released as a 'special,' " the Story Department's notice continued, "so we are naturally hopeful of a special response to the attached outline. It offers a challenge to the best imaginations on the lot. Please *give*."

As was Walt's way, the Story Department then gave a synopsis of the story, followed by a list of twenty questions designed to stimulate imaginations all over the lot into writing (or, preferably, drawing) answers to such queries as: What could Mickey do with the stars in the heavens? What transition do you see from the dream back to reality and Mickey's predicament? What tie-in between water in the dream and the water actually in the room?

From the beginning Walt described *The Sorcerer's Apprentice* to his staff in terms that would later apply to the whole of *Fantasia*: he called it a "musical fantasy offering an opportunity for a new type of entertainment," adding that "the picture will be made without dialogue and without sound effects, depending solely on pantomime and the descriptive music," and asking his staff to "please avoid slapstick gags in the ordinary sense; work instead toward fantasy and business with an imaginative touch. . . ."

Like all Disney directors, Jim Algar was an always-on-the-job extension of Walt's overall supervision of everything. As such he was present through the night of January 9-10, 1938, when Leopold Stokowski and a full orchestra of hand-picked musicians (but not the Philadelphia Orchestra) recorded *The Sorcerer's Apprentice*. Algar remembered "Stokowski's recording session for *Sorcerer* at 12:00 midnight to 3:00 A.M. in a big soundstage on the Selznick lot (the Hyperion Avenue soundstage wasn't large enough), with cables and wires running every which way to the sound trucks outside. . . . One rehearsal and Stokowski galvanized eighty-five musicians to a pitch of tenseness that produced in three short hours the complete seven-track recording of Dukas's music, then stepped down soaked with perspiration from head to foot. No mere handkerchief could mop his steaming brow: he was handed two man-sized bath towels. The reason Stokowski preferred recording at 3:00 A.M.? 'The men drink coffee to keep awake; it makes everybody alert.' "

Roy Disney, Walt's business manager brother, was sweating, too, as he watched the costs mount on this two-reel short to $125,000.

One of the chief reasons Walt was able to sell Roy on the untried idea of a concert feature was, according to Ben Sharpsteen, that *The Sorcerer's Apprentice* "had cost three or four times as much as a Silly Symphony should have cost. We realized that we could never get our money back on it. Walt—and this was a big factor with Walt,

STOKISAURUS

NOTE DOUBLE
TAIL

how alert he was to opportunities—saw this trouble in the form of an opportunity."

Sharpsteen described how Walt's thought processes led him to the idea of a concert feature:

" 'This thing can't earn its money back this way. How can we merchandise it so it *will* make money? Here's an idea!' Quality came first in his opinion; the box office will follow quality. This was the birth of a new concept, a group of separate numbers, regardless of their running time, put together in a single presentation. Instead of calling it a vaudeville show, it turned out to be a concert—something novel and of high quality."

It has been written that the idea of expanding the film from *The Sorcerer's Apprentice* to a concert feature was Stokowski's, but that is not what Stokowski recalled. "When it [*Sorcerer*] was almost finished," he wrote, "Walt said to me: 'Why don't we make a bigger picture with all kinds of music?' and that led to *Fantasia*."

Stokowski returned to the Disney Studio early in September, 1938. Joining him to act as musical adviser on the concert feature was Deems Taylor, who had composed the first American opera ever presented at the Metropolitan Opera House, *The King's Henchman*, in 1927, with a libretto by Edna St. Vincent Millay, and who was then well known to a national radio audience as the intermission commentator for the New York Philharmonic Symphony radio broadcasts. Taylor wrote and delivered the spoken introductions to all the selections on the *Fantasia* program. (On the 1982 digital sound track, Taylor's introductions are spoken by someone else.)

Walt picked two of his artists, Dick Huemer and Joe Grant, to make a preliminary selection of music that might be suitable for animation. The happy-go-lucky Huemer had been an animator and director for Disney before Walt discovered his gift for story (he and Grant would later work out the screen story for *Dumbo*) and Huemer loved music of all kinds. "Meet Dick Huemer; he goes to operas," was the way Walt often introduced him. As head of Disney's Character Model Department, Grant had designed the Wicked Queen for *Snow White*, and he had a talent for imagining personalities in anything— including music.

In September, 1938, Disney, Stokowski, Taylor, Grant, Huemer, and the heads of various Disney departments got together for a three-week conference at which hundreds of recordings were played and the concert feature program was picked. Stokowski, sharpening the focus on Disney's "musical fantasy," called their project a "fantasia," which is a musical term for a composition in a fanciful or irregular form or style. It was just a working title, but its universality appealed to everybody— *fantasia* means *fantasia* in every language— and it stuck.

Stokowski, who made his first phonograph record in 1917, was a pioneer among conductors in his dedication to the improvement of recorded sound. In Walt Disney, who always wanted to be the first to use any technological advance, he found a kindred spirit. Disney and Stokowski agreed that the playback of Stokowski's recording of *The Sorcerer's Apprentice* did not—could not—duplicate the full, rich orchestral sound heard on the sound stage. Disney assigned Bill

Garity and the Walt Disney Studio Sound Department to develop a new system of multiaural sound that could create a more convincing illusion of a live performance.

Stokowski understood that "recording for motion pictures . . . cannot possibly sound exactly like the original because the original sounds from the orchestra came from a hundred different instruments and directions, whereas the reproduced music in the motion picture house comes from a relatively small number of sound diffusers or loudspeakers. In the original version of *Fantasia* we diffused the sound in two ways—one was from back of the screen from three separate groups of loudspeakers—left, center, right—the other was from loudspeakers all round the theater. . . . In *Fantasia* we had three separate sound channels, which put at our disposal several new possibilities. When the sound waves of all the instruments are combined in a single channel, they often interfere with each other and cause cross-modulation, which makes the music sound distorted. With three separate channels, it is possible to send out the music on each channel from relatively few instruments. This reduces cross-modulation and gives greater purity to the sound of the instruments. Another great advantage of three sound channels is that the tone of the various instruments can be blended in the air after the sound has left the speakers. This corresponds somewhat to the blending of colors in *pointillisme*, the method of painting in which the colors are not mixed on the canvas, but are blended in the space between the canvas and our eyes as we look at the picture."

Disney called the result of the research Fantasound. To get the best possible quality, Walt had Stokowski record all the music in *Fantasia* (except *The Sorcerer's Apprentice*, which had already been recorded in Hollywood) at the venerable Philadelphia Academy of Music, legendary for its superb acoustics. There, Abraham Lincoln had spoken, Jenny Lind had sung, and Stokowski had drawn the sounds from his Philadelphia Orchestra, making them world-famous.

"You know, we had nine separate sound tracks in *Fantasia*," said Dick Huemer, who was among the group of story directors, studio musicians, and technicians that Disney took to Philadelphia. "So we had nine separate command posts in the basement of the theater, each one recording one of the sound tracks from its own mike placed in a different spot. And I remember that in the basement, right underneath the audience, was a big, round brick wall. Across the top of this there were stringers or beams very much like the sounding board of an instrument. I guess the architect's idea was that the theater would reverberate like a huge instrument or something—and maybe it does, because those acoustics are famous.

"One night when we finished, Walt said, 'Where should we go to eat?' Now I was a New Yorker. I'd been to Philadelphia. And Bookbinder's is one of its most famous restaurants. So I suggested Bookbinder's. And Walt loved the place. After that, it wasn't, 'Meet Dick Huemer; he knows all about opera.' It was, 'Meet Dick Huemer; he knows all the best restaurants in Philadelphia.' But that tells you an important thing about Walt: it was important to him to know what you knew—and he always remembered."

*"Happy-go-lucky Dick Huemer,"* Time *magazine called him. Huemer became a top Disney storyman because he shared Walt's passion for analyzing stories until it was understood clearly how a real-life situation could be exaggerated to present an entertaining animated caricature of life on the screen. Disney teamed Huemer and Joe Grant, head of his Character Model Department, as story directors for Fantasia, but Huemer always insisted that "Walt was his own best storyman."*

*Walt Disney sits with Igor Stravinsky, the only living composer on the* Fantasia *program, and examines the score for* Rite of Spring *just before Christmas, 1939.*

Stokowski seemed to have as much fun listening to the sound as Walt had seeing to the visuals. John Hench, who was working in Story Development at the time, remembers that "Stokowski was fascinated by the mixing board—the sound control panel. For *Fantasia* he recorded each section separately—strings, winds, horns, etc. —and he mixed them all himself. He said this was the ultimate in conducting: he could dial up the strings or turn down the others, getting exact mixtures of sounds. With the panel he could control the entire orchestra. That little board on the Hyperion Avenue Studio's sound stage gave him a great sense of power."

The results were unique. "For example," Stokowski wrote in *Music for All of Us,* "in the thunderstorm part of Beethoven's *Pastoral Symphony* are certain intense phrases for bassoon, clarinet, and oboe, which have an urgent, agitated expression. These phrases are almost inaudible in the concert hall because the rest of the orchestra is playing loudly and furiously. In *Fantasia* we were able to give these important passages their true value by making the melodic lines for bassoon, clarinet, and oboe soar above the rest of the orchestra without emasculating the rushing stormy music of all the string instruments. Because of the inherent lack of balance in the orchestration, I have never before heard these phrases given their due prominence and tonal importance."

Stokowski had recorded each section of the orchestra individually, then mixed the nine separate optical tracks that resulted on four master tracks. These tracks were heard by the audience for Fantasound from three sound horns behind the picture screen instead of the usual one, plus sixty-five small house-speakers placed strategically throughout the auditorium. Thus, when a muted horn in *Rite of Spring* heralds the approach of Tyrannosaurus Rex, the horn sounds from the auditorium, far from the screen. As the monster comes closer to the screen, so does the horn call. When he crashes into the clearing, there is a crashing dissonance issuing from the very point on the screen where he appears.

The adventure that was the making of *Fantasia* lasted about three years, from the preparation of a rough continuity for *The Sorcerer's Apprentice* in November, 1937, to the cliff-hanger finish of camera work on the *Ave Maria* two days before the world premiere in November, 1940. It must have been one of the most exuberant periods in the history of film art. The *Atlantic Monthly* sent Paul Hollister to the Studio to write "Walt Disney: Genius at Work," and he asked Bill Tytla, one of Disney's greatest animators, why people liked to work there.

Tytla "tousled his hair, scowled hard into his Coke to aid thinking, and answered: 'You know, you and I have seen some outfits that *had* it. They had *something.* The thing here is like that—you know, you can't help feeling that you're going to grab that goddam Holy Grail. That sounds terrible. I just can't express it exactly.' "

No one could express it, exactly, but all kinds of artists felt that something big was happening and dropped by the Disney Studio

*Disney listens to Stokowski record for* Fantasia *at Philadelphia's Academy of Music. The music bill alone amounted to more than $400,000 of* Fantasia*'s total cost of $2,280,000. Walt's suspenders are a switch from his customary belted slacks, but the cigarette burning in the ashtray is typical.*

to watch. Walt greeted them in an office where the windowsills, desktop, bookshelves, and the top of the grand piano formed a route for a parade of full-color ceramic statuettes. In those days, his Character Model Department didn't just produce two-dimensional model sheets to guide the animators; they sculpted three-dimensional clay models that were then painted and glazed, so that the animators could see their characters in the round, from all angles. Very often Walt found himself giving these statuettes to visiting VIPs.

When members of the Association of American Artists visited the Studio, pipe-puffing Thomas Hart Benton posed with a little centaur from *The Pastoral Symphony,* and Grant Wood grinned at a centaurette. Kirsten Flagstad, the century's greatest Wagnerian soprano, was photographed with Walt and the same centaurette. Maude Adams, who originated the role of Peter Pan in James M. Barrie's play, was shown Freddy Moore's model sheets of Mickey Mouse as the Sorcerer's apprentice, and Katharine Cornell, another of the century's greatest actresses, held Hyacinth Hippo as she studied model sheets of unicorns. Another statuette of Hyacinth in her tutu brought smiles to the faces of choreographer George Balanchine and Igor Stravinsky, the great composer, who came to the Studio together at Christmas of 1939 to see the models and model sheets and hear the sound track for Stravinsky's *Rite of Spring.* Dr. Edwin Hubble of the Mt. Wilson Observatory and Dr. Julian Huxley, the author and biologist, also studied the models and model sheets for the Stravinsky sequence and expressed their appreciation of the Studio's efforts on behalf of prehistoric authenticity. A wave of excitement went through the Studio, and some artists dreamed of *Rite of Spring* being shown one day in schools—which it now is. Novelist and Nobel laureate Thomas Mann looked at *Sorcerer* storyboards and pointed out that Goethe, a subject of his recent book *Three Essays,* had written the poem *Der Zauberlehrling (The Apprentice Magician),* on which Dukas based his music.

By the time *Fantasia* was in production two cels (celluloids on which the animated figures were painted) from *Snow White* were in the collection of the Metropolitan Museum of Art in New York. Yet the artists at the Disney Studio understood almost to a man that theirs was a kinetic art, and no still painting or sequence of drawings could ever represent what that art really was when projected at twenty-four frames a second.

Animation began on January 21, 1938, when Jim Algar, as director, assigned Preston Blair the scene in *The Sorcerer's Apprentice* in which Mickey wakes from his dream, and continued until the retakes were completed on *Ave Maria* in November of 1940; through it all there was a terrific concentration on the one aspect of graphic art that could never be explored before animation: how things *moved.*

Specifically, the word "animation" is used to designate the creation of artificial movement by cinematic synthesis. In any kind of cinema (a word derived from the Greek word for movement) what we see is really only a series of still pictures. These static images that were photographed on a long reel of film are projected by a beam of light onto a screen at the rate of twenty-four images, or "frames,"

Kirsten Flagstad, the century's greatest Wagnerian soprano, poses with models for Dance of the Hours and The Pastoral Symphony. Madame Flagstad holds a centaurette that is half zebra and half human. The human half was designed to be bare breasted, but the Hays Office, Hollywood's censorship organization, insisted on garlands, or at least a pair of flowers, for modesty's sake (opposite, above).

T. Hee, caricaturist and co-director of Dance of the Hours, shows a model sheet of unicorns for The Pastoral Symphony to actress Katharine Cornell. Her attention is focused on the star of Dance of the Hours, Hyacinth Hippo (opposite, below).

Standing before a storyboard, Walt Disney shows a model of Mlle. Upanova, the ostrich ballerina, to choreographer George Balanchine and composer Igor Stravinsky (left).

The Association of American Artists visited the Studio in a body (above). Studying models of Fantasia characters are (left to right): George Biddle, A.A.A. director Reeves Lewenthal, Thomas Hart Benton, Ernest Fiene, Grant Wood, and Georges Schreiber.

per second. At this rate, because of a phenomenon known as the persistence of vision, the luminous impression of each image upon our eyes lasts until the next image supplants it. In consequence, we experience the illusion of seeing continuous movement. Watching separate images of Mickey Mouse waving, for example, our eyes are still taking in the drawing of Mickey with his hand down when we see the drawing of Mickey with his hand up, so our brain thinks that it has just seen the drawing of Mickey wave. To make an animated cartoon of any length, therefore, the artist draws and photographs the successive phases of its actions much as a live-action camera would automatically record them, but he caricatures these actions to make them convincing despite their lack of realistic detail. This is why Walt Disney called his medium "a caricature of life."

Walt had finally refined his Studio's approach to the making of the twenty-four images needed for every second of screen time until it was the efficient, nine-step operation that produced, between 1934 and 1942, the five great Disney features: *Snow White, Pinocchio, Fantasia, Dumbo,* and *Bambi.* There was actually a flow chart where the steps were called *Walt, Story, Sound, Director, Layout, Animation, Background, Inking and Painting,* and *Camera,* and that's pretty much how all those pictures were made.

Walt and the artists in his Story Department would originate and develop the ideas that formed the basis of Disney's pictures and, like *Fantasia,* they were often Disney's ideas. His story artists would explore these subjects in sketch form, making small drawings in colored pencil portraying various situations and gags that might add up to a good theme, a smooth continuity, a compelling plot. As animator and storyman Frank Thomas slyly put it: "The challenge to the storyman was how to make a rich, colorful, complicated story of great philosophic importance in six or seven simple little happy sequences with a mixture of awesome fantasy and great comedy." When these sketches were tacked up in sequence on the storyboards, they were studied in relation to the story as a whole. When the story artists decided that a board was ready, it would be acted out for Walt by a storyteller who pointed to the appropriate sketch and tried to suggest with his voice and his body movements what the animator could do with it. At these meetings, Walt and the other viewers were expected to pitch in enthusiastically to strengthen the story with their own ideas. So Mickey Mouse bringing the broom to life and leading him to the well would start out with a story artist making a sketch of those actions for the storyboard and then acting out for Walt and the story staff — and eventually for the director Walt was assigning to the picture — just how somebody with Mickey's personality might perform such actions.

Ordinarily, when Walt gave his okay to a storyboard, the dialogue and sound effects that were called for would be recorded, and composers and lyricists would start working on the songs and the musical score. In *Fantasia,* of course, there was no dialogue or sound effects, and the music was recorded before animation began.

Walt would give the approved storyboards to a director, who would assign the various scenes to his animators. The director would rehearse the action of his sequence with them; guide them in their interpretation of each individual scene in relation to the picture as a whole; designate the music, dialogue, and sound effects to be used; and supervise the cutting and staging. He was also supposed to improve the storyboards (Walt called it "plussing" them) by giving the characters gestures that would make their personalities more believable, and by adding gags and developing continuity. And he was supposed to answer all the questions of the animators and make all the final decisions in connection with his sequence. Of course, he could always be second-guessed by Walt.

Working with the director, the story layout artist was responsible for the graphic development of each scene, which meant researching and then executing the locales and props in detail and in perspective, and giving them the most effective camera angles and moods. He planned the exact size of each scene, the general color schemes, and all the working details of the backgrounds and characters. He was responsible for the plan of action that the animator followed in relation to the background and the music. So he had to understand action and be able to give the animator characters that "worked" and scenes in which the action was possible.

In effect, the director "saw" the story in time and the layout artist saw it in space. When the story was ready for actual animation, the director would make out an exposure sheet, a long sheet of paper on which every horizontal line represented one frame of film. Using this sheet the director could choreograph the actions in time by showing the animator exactly how many drawings he wanted him to use to create an action on the screen. The layout man, on the other hand, would choreograph the actions in space by giving the animator layout drawings made in blue pencil that showed him the spatial relationships of everything in the setting and what general paths of action his characters had to follow lest they walk through props. For example, layout man Zack Schwartz gave animator Les Clark drawings of the courtyard where Mickey was to command the broom to fill the buckets and the path that Mickey and the broom would follow from the courtyard down the stairway to the vat in the Sorcerer's gloomy cavern. And the director told Clark how he wanted Mickey to lead the broom: "He turns and starts, sergeantlike, but kidlike he looks back to see if it's still working, and yes it is." The director had shot live action of a child leading an imaginary broom, and he showed it to Clark. "I like the way the kid in the live action handles his elbows, arms, and head," he said. But then he exhorted Clark to give him far more in animating Mickey than there was in the live action of the boy playing the apprentice. "You can get a whale of a lot of spirit in Mickey marching along there. You know, he feels he's some punkin—let him step high, wide, and handsome, like an Elk on parade."

Inevitably, no matter how careful the preparation, the animator would finally find himself alone in his room with a blank sheet of paper, like the princess in the fairy tale who must spin straw into gold. The story could only reach the screen through what he put on that paper, and there is no record of Rumpelstiltskin ever helping an animator. Walt constantly reminded everyone that the ultimate suc-

*Walt decided to "plus" Mickey in* The Sorcerer's Apprentice *and "Mickey expert" Fred Moore was called in to help redesign the Mouse. He gave Mickey pupils in his eyes for the first time to increase his range of expression, as in this guilty upward glance at the Sorcerer. It was also decided to let the broom straws part to look like flippers, so that the broom could walk like a seal.*

Layout head same as ever | Place eyes on each side of middle line

Use black above new eyes as eye brows.

COMPARATIVE
SIZES OF
BROOM,
BUCKET AND MICKEY

cess of all his stories depended upon that solitary pencil-pusher's ability to dramatize personality in action. Disney's sketch artists could develop the story with appealing pictures of Mickey leading a broom; the director could conceive its timing, acting, and continuity; the layout man design its setting and give it its sense of scale; but unless the animator made you care, the picture would be a beautiful bore. "In our animation," said Walt, "we must show not only the actions or reactions of a character, but we must picture also with the action . . . the *feeling* of those characters."

By making a series of pencil drawings of the successive phases of each action, the animator animated his scene. And he hoped that, projected at the proper speed, those drawings would give

# The SORCERER'S APPRENTICE
## RX-1

| DIRECTOR | ALGAR |
|---|---|
| STORY | PERCE |
| ANIMATOR | & Moore |
| LAYOUT | Godwich |

Philippi
Dike

Draw stars
and crescent
to fit the
contour of
hat.

RETAIN MICKEY BODY UNDER CLOAK

Original animation drawings from The Sorcerer's Apprentice.

not only the illusion that we were seeing the same actions that he visualized in his imagination, but also a character who was feeling and thinking as well as moving. We can see the inspirational drawings that Les Clark started with showing Mickey leading the broom, as well as some of the animation drawings he made, but we can only see on the screen the spirit with which he imbued Mickey Mouse in motion. Mickey skipped about to the musical beat with a hippity-hop action that is the essence of Mickey's jaunty little-boy determination. He hopped down the stairs backward. He bowed the broom through the courtyard. He did a cakewalk down the steps, among the vats, and over to the Sorcerer's chair, into which he flopped, and then, with supreme self-confidence, stuck his feet up on the table and continued conducting the actions of the broom with his hands.

And that is what a good animator does: he creates a semblance of movement that causes us to suspend disbelief. And so, in animation rooms all over the Studio during the making of *Fantasia*, these "actors with pencils," as animators are often called, were digging into their psyches and trying to imagine the dumb despair a dinosaur shows when it knows it is going to die; how the smallest mushroom in a group moves when he is trying to get in step; how the god of evil reacts when he realizes that the power of good is too strong for him; and how Mickey Mouse shows his feelings when he realizes that he has brought a broom to life. They had lots of advice, of course, from Walt to the story artists to the director and layout man, to their fellow animators who made drawings for them; but, finally, it was pretty much like giving Fred Astaire advice on how to do a tap dance. Only he could move the arms and legs.

Much of the atmosphere in which all these dramas are enacted is provided by the background paintings. Think of the contrast between the light, sunny courtyard where the broom gets the water and the Sorcerer's gloomy cavern where things go out of control. Such backgrounds were executed in transparent watercolor, with attention paid to the psychological effects of color to intensify the details, props, and atmospheric effects indicated in the layout artist's design.

The animator's drawings were traced onto cels by inkers (since 1960, they have been Xeroxed onto cels), then painted on the reverse side by painters using predetermined colors manufactured and patented by the studio. Each cel was then sent with its appropriate background to the camera department. Together, these "cel set-ups" were photographed one frame at a time onto a continuous roll of film.

Many *Fantasia* scenes were photographed on Disney's legendary multiplane camera, which was developed to give the illusion of depth to scenes in *Snow White* and won a special Academy Award in 1937 for its design and application to production.

Even as the premiere of *Fantasia* loomed ahead, the Disney Studio developed a horizontal multiplane camera on which to shoot the long procession of pilgrims that Walt envisioned for the *Ave Maria* finale. Such an experiment was typical of the Studio in its Golden Age, when every possibility of the process of animation was being meticulously explored.

But the primary emphasis was always on how things moved. "How do you see the dewdrops forming?" story artist Bianca Majolie asked Walt one day, when she was sketching up the tiny fairies waving their wands in the Sugar Plum sequence of *The Nutcracker Suite.* "I think they roll out of their wands," Walt answered. "One dewdrop could land and a whole string of drops run off. I wouldn't complicate it — I think they should be flying around and several of them converge and sprinkle this spider web. . . ."

It was his genius to imagine how things might look and sound and move, particularly move; and often they were things that neither he nor anybody else had ever seen before. In another part of the Studio, animation directors asked the impossible of Margie Belcher, an inventive dancer who later became famous as Marge Champion, and transmuted her inspired responses into movements for ostrich ballerinas and dancing blossoms. Elsewhere, the 115-pound actor who had modeled for Jiminy Cricket in the award-winning *Pinocchio* now pretended he was Zeus, throwing lightning bolts at Bacchus from a cloud, while a chubby man posed for the hindquarters of a centaur. Meanwhile, a young artist named John Hench had sneered at ballet dancers in Walt's hearing; Walt arranged for Hench to watch the Ballet Russe from backstage as he had formerly arranged to have vaudeville tickets to Joe Jackson & His Bicycle for animators working on the Seven Dwarfs, so that they would think in terms of stylized movements. Hench returned with drawings for the *Nutcracker Suite* that benefited from his exposure to the dance — as well as the beginnings of friendships with dancers that have lasted a lifetime.

And then, suddenly, it was all over. *Fantasia* was in the can. Walt's voyage of discovery brought him into port in New York at the Broadway Theater where, before the opening night, he flopped sideways into a seat, lifted his legs over the armrest and stretched them into the next seat, ran his hand through his hair, and listened as they tested the sound for *Night on Bald Mountain.* He was very nervous.

"I never liked this stuff," he admitted to a reporter from the New York *World-Telegram* about classical music. "Honest, I just couldn't listen to it. But I can listen to it now. It seems to mean a little more to me. Maybe it can give other people the same thing. When I heard the music it made pictures in my head. Then the boys listened and they had ideas. I had a lot of ideas, but they voted some of them down. Anyway, here are the pictures. . . .

"Stravinsky saw his *Rite of Spring* and said that that was what he had in mind all the time. None of that matters, I guess. This isn't a picture just for music lovers. People have to like it. They have to be entertained. We're selling entertainment and that's the thing I'm hoping *Fantasia* does — entertain. I'm hoping, hoping, hoping."

Storms that had been sweeping eastward since the beginning of that week brought rain that fell on New York City on and off all Wednesday, November 13, the day of the premiere, then suddenly stopped just before the theater opened. Huck Finn put on a tux and became Tom Sawyer for the premiere.

"Motion picture history was made last night," wrote Bosley Crowther in the *New York Times,* praising *Fantasia* as a film that "dumps conventional formulas overboard and reveals the scope of films for imaginative excursion. . . . *Fantasia* . . . is simply terrific."

From the beginning, most film critics, art critics, and dance critics shared the view of Otis Ferguson of the *New Republic* that *Fantasia* was "one of the strange and beautiful things that have happened in the world."

*Dance* magazine devoted its lead article to the film, saying that "the extraordinary thing about *Fantasia* is, to a dancer or a balletomane, not the miraculous musical recording, the complete range of color, or the fountainous ingenuity of the Disney collaborators, but quite simply the perfection of its dancing."

The *Art Digest* ran a signed editorial by its editor and publisher, Peyton Boswell, calling *Fantasia* "an aesthetic experience never to be forgotten. Compressed within this new art form — for that is the designation that must be accorded the latest of the animated films — are extracted essences from all the older arts, given realization through the imagination and magic of Disney's genius."

The most significant dissenters were the music critics. In general they objected to *Fantasia*'s basic notion of coexpressing so-called "classical" music with *any* visual complement. Virgil Thompson, the composer and critic, applauded the sound (". . . once the public has heard a good transmission of music, I doubt if it will ever again be satisfied with poor") but denigrated "Mr. Stokowski's musical taste" — except in *The Sorcerer's Apprentice* and *Rite of Spring.*

"Only the geology lesson to Stravinsky's fine score is in any way superior to the famous Silly Symphony of several years back in which Donald Duck conducted the *William Tell Overture,*" wrote Thompson, remembering *The Band Concert* but confusing Donald Duck with Mickey Mouse.

In the Sunday *New York Times,* music critic Olin Downes wrote a long and closely reasoned essay on "Disney's Experiment." "Musicians and music lovers as a class were thrilled by the quality of the tone transmission, as was the writer," he said. But he felt that much of *Fantasia* distracted from or directly injured the scores. He recalled that "the last great artistic synthesis" of sight and sound "was that achieved in the first decade of this century by the original Diaghilev ballet," and he analyzed in detail the way that Fokine's choreography for Rimsky-Korsakov's *Scheherazade*—which did not follow at all the composer's captions in the score—was nevertheless "a companion creation of a parallel character which completed and did not belie the nature of the score. . . .

"For all that," Downes concluded, Disney's "initial attempt is invaluable. It opens a field in which he and others will advance and create wonder. And then comes the next step for which we all wait and pray, the advent of the great American composer, the Stravinsky, if you like . . . to companion the genius of the movies."

But there were to be no more experiments like *Fantasia* for Walt Disney. We can see now that the film was a victim of World War II. It tells what the times were that the proceeds from the premiere of *Fantasia* went to British War Relief, for the Battle of Britain, in which Hitler tried and failed to achieve his dream of invading England, had ended only thirteen days before. Thirteen months later the United States came into the war. The artist who had used the money that *Snow White*'s success brought him to build the most modern film studio in the world was faced first with the cutoff of his European markets (45 percent of his income), and then by the diminished popularity in time of war of such gentle fantasies as *Pinocchio, Fantasia,* and *Bambi.* (All three would eventually rank, in less bellicose times, among the most popular films in history.) Disney and his Studio survived by making propaganda films for the government and training films for the military until peace came again.

In New York, *Fantasia* ran at the Broadway Theater for a year. Elsewhere in the country, *Fantasia* met resistance from patrons who complained that it was different from other Disney films and from parents who balked at paying roadshow prices for children. In any case, electronic equipment was needed by the government for the war effort. The costly Fantasound installations for *Fantasia* were abandoned in 1941.

Walt had intended that the reproduction of *Fantasia*'s music would always be state-of-the-art for its time. "After the two and a half years which went into the making of *Fantasia,*" said a press release that Disney put out with his film, "Disney and Stokowski feel that it is not a finished product but an indication of the great possibilities the future may develop in this new entertainment medium. . . . *Fantasia* is not the final expression of this new union of color and music and action. It is the beginning of a new treatment and technique for the screen, as well as an indication of the greater development of sound recording and reproduction."

In 1956, flushed with the success of Disneyland the year before, Walt reissued the film a second time—with the original optical Fantasound tracks rechanneled on four-track magnetic film, with the fourth track emanating from speakers in the auditorium. (Optical sound tracks are produced on photographic film with photographic means, then modulations are electrically converted from light impulses to audible sound during projection. In magnetic recording, the sound is reproduced by magnetic means on tape or film with an iron oxide coating. Magnetic recording is usually accomplished in synchronization with motion picture film and later transferred by optical means to photographic film.) It was the magnetic version, with at least some of the fidelity and spread of Fantasound, that first transformed *Fantasia* into a money-maker.

Then came 1969, and a new generation embraced the film, at least partially for new reasons. The twenty-nine-year-old film was now seen as a psychedelic experience.

Since then *Fantasia* has earned the Disney organization about $2 million a year—every year. But the sound track recorded in 1938 has steadily deteriorated, despite a simulated stereo version in 1977. So in 1981 Walt Disney Productions decided to give *Fantasia* the first digitally recorded motion picture score, thereby making it state-of-the-art once more.

Digital technology measures sound and then converts the measurements into a series of numbers (or digits). The series is stored on a tape memory, then reconverted into accurate reproductions of the original sound measurements by a computer that generates a normal audio signal. The advantages: as many copies as are needed can be made from the digital original with no error, no distortion, and virtually no loss of quality, and the frequency response is accurate from zero to the highest recordable frequency.

For the rerecording of *Fantasia*, the new digital technique was used in conjunction with the patented Dolby noise-reduction method. The result is sound that emerges from a deep silence with the same clarity as Disney's colors: there is no machine noise, no hiss, nothing except the pure sounds of the orchestra itself.

The conductor who rerecorded the score of *Fantasia* was Irwin Kostal, who won Oscars for his musical supervision of *West Side Story* and *The Sound of Music*. But it is still, for the most part, the Stokowski interpretation of the pieces played.

"Whoever agrees to walk in Stokowski's footsteps, as it were, must also accept Stokowski's straitjacket," wrote Martin Bernheimer in the *Los Angeles Times*. "The new *Fantasia* may boast state-of-the-art stereo advantages, complete with Dolby and digital devices, but it can provide the maestro-in-residence with few independent options. Tempos and cuts have been predetermined. Accents are dictated, further, by the movements of the figures in the film. The new *Fantasia* conductor must be a master of timing and matching and cueing. That is ultimately more important than being a master at interpreting Bach and Beethoven."

What Kostal could certainly achieve, on the centenary of Stokowski's birth, was a recording fidelity that Stokowski, though he had died only five years before, never knew. For the *Night on Bald Mountain* sequence, Kostal used Moussorgsky's own, wild orchestration rather than the tamer Rimsky-Korsakov scoring that Stokowski thought 1940 audiences would be more likely to accept.

"We can go from zero to ninety decibels and really rock the theater, if we want to," said Kostal, "with no distortion."

In the digital *Night on Bald Mountain*, Kostal achieves the apotheosis of *Walpurgisnacht*—and it's likely that if Stokowski and Disney could have heard it, Stokowski and Mickey Mouse would both have shaken Kostal's hand.

The famous moment when Mickey shakes hands with "Mr. Stokowski" and offers the maestro "my congratulations, sir!" on his conducting of *The Sorcerer's Apprentice* remains in the film, and that's fitting. For the digital *Fantasia* is just the latest development in the evolution of a film that began when Disney and Stokowski collaborated on a special short called *The Sorcerer's Apprentice* and that grew into the concert feature we know today as *Fantasia*.

"That word 'evolution,' I keep using that," said Ben Sharpsteen in discussing *Fantasia*, "but it applies so much to Walt's practice—that one thing evolved from another and sometimes things played out and died on a dead end street—but oftentimes it led to something else, and . . . the making of *Fantasia* was one of those kinds of progressive evolutions."

*In 1940,* Fantasia *was the first film to be released with stereophonic sound. In 1938, live-action film crews photographed human characters for the first time on the Disney lot, for the orchestral sequence that introduced the film (opposite). First to go before the camera was Leopold Stokowski. In 1982,* Fantasia *was the first film to be recorded, edited, and dubbed in digital audio. Irwin Kostal (above), who won Academy Awards for adapting the music in* West Side Story *and* The Sound of Music, *conducted the new sound track based on Stokowski's original one.*

# TOCCATA AND FUGUE

*The live-action film of the orchestra that was being shot on the preceding page looked like this on the screen.*

# IN D MINOR

Toccata and Fugue in D Minor was written for the organ by Johann Sebastian Bach between 1703 and 1717. The symphonic transcription was orchestrated as well as conducted by Leopold Stokowski. The Disney version is a pictorial description of the form of the music. A toccata is fantasialike music in a free style, while a fugue interweaves several musical themes in a strict pattern. So Disney begins by improvising with images that are Technicolor impressions of the orchestra in performance. We see Stokowski walk up to the podium, call the orchestra to attention with his hands (he never used a baton), and start conducting against a background that responds to the music by darkening from cobalt blue to dark maroon. The podium as a mountainlike dais, giving prominence to whoever occupies it, is a motif that will recur throughout the film—the actual conductor's podium up which Mickey Mouse runs to shake Stokowski's hand; the mountaintop from which Mickey conducts the stars and planets; Bald Mountain, from which the devil conducts the Walpurgis Night dance of the damned. Real or fanciful, it is the central image of *Fantasia*.

What we see on the screen are pictures of the shifting abstract images that might pass before the mind's eye as we sit in a concert hall listening to this music. At first, we are more or less conscious of the orchestra, so the *Toccata* begins with images that are impressions of the orchestra itself: multiple shadows of nine violinists accompany a violin passage; triple red shadows of cellists on a blue background appear when the cellos are heard; three French horns are seen in silhouette, and light up when they play; a harp glows gold against blue.

The *Fugue* begins, and the images become less and less concrete. The theme repeats seven times in the course of the *Fugue*, and each time the graphic form changes with the development of the musical theme. Abstract music is reflected visually in abstract images that resemble both violin bows and swallows, and flit like swallows; musical calls and answers are interpreted as changes of color washing over the screen or as moving spots of color, or as string bass shapes calling and their shadows answering. Shafts of light build up on a black screen until they, too, suggest the recurring podium image. Interestingly, the end of *Fantasia*'s first number is an abstraction of the end of *Fantasia*'s final number. In the *Fugue*, cloud forms suggest a Gothic cathedral as trees will do in the *Ave Maria;* there is an abstract hint in the Bach of a shattered stained glass window falling that will be echoed later in the Schubert when light assumes the shape of a cathedral window. The Bach concludes with a sunset and columns of light that suggest the pipes of an organ, a foreshadowing of the Schubert ending where the predawn sky is filled with color by a sunrise.

**Y**ou will be able to SEE the music and HEAR the picture," said Walt Disney of his hopes for *Fantasia*; and you can read, in excerpts from the transcripts of their story meetings, how Disney and Stokowski and their associates worked toward achieving that aim.

In a story meeting on the *Toccata and Fugue* held on Tuesday afternoon, November 8, 1938, John McLeish, a story artist with the manner of John Barrymore (his stentorian tones can be heard narrating the opening of *Dumbo*), began talking about the "contrast between the screen and the music." In the *Fugue,* suggested McLeish, why not "picture a huge form moving slowly against a counterpoint in the music? Or just the opposite, when you have a slow, heavy chord, picture little, light forms playing against that."

Stokowski was in immediate agreement. "When there is counterpoint in the music," he said, "there should be counterpoint in the picture. The music explains the screen, and the screen explains the music. We must make it clear."

Much of the strength of Disney's images came from their clarity and simplicity, so Disney now knew where he wanted to go with the studio's visualization of the *Toccata and Fugue in D Minor* by Johann Sebastian Bach.

"There are things in that music that the general public will not understand until they see things on the screen representing that music," said Disney. "Then they will feel the depth in the music. Our object is to reach the very people who have walked out on this *Toccata and Fugue* because they didn't understand it. I am one of those people; but when I understand it, I like it."

Sir Herbert Read, in *Art and Alienation,* called Walt Disney a "great expressionist," but Disney was a storyteller first and foremost; so the aim of Abstract Expressionism, which seeks to express feeling and emotion solely through color and nonobjective or nonrepresentational form, was secondary to his most important aim of developing definite personalities in his cartoon characters. Nonetheless he was experimenting with various combinations of music and pictures in *Fantasia,* and Stokowski and Deems Taylor had told him that there are three kinds of music: music that tells a story, such as *The Sorcerer's Apprentice*; music that paints a picture, such as *The Pastoral Symphony,* with its musical portrait of nature; and "absolute music," or music for music's sake.

Disney said that he had been interested in abstract films since he saw Len Lye's animated abstract film, *Colour Box,* in the mid-1930s. "There was an Englishman named Len Lye who did color and movement to music," wrote Disney. "He applied this directly on film by painting on the film itself." And Stokowski had once conducted an experimental concert which combined the music of the Philadelphia Orchestra with a color organ. So Disney decided to make the first selection on the *Fantasia* program a further experiment in interpreting the tone colors and sound patterns of music in the colors and moving patterns on the screen.

"The *Toccata and Fugue* was chosen," said the program, "not only because it is magnificent music but also because it lends itself to this type of interpretation—it being music which neither seeks to tell a story nor paint a picture, but exists solely for the beauty of its own tone patterns."

Disney himself explained, in 1944: "The abstractions that were done in *Toccata and Fugue* were no sudden idea. Rather, they were something we had nursed along for several years but we never had a chance to try due to the fact that the type of pictures being made up to that time did not allow us to incorporate any of this type of material in them. Actually, it was an outgrowth of our Effects Department which we organized long before we had any contact with Stokowski.

"The idea of color and music is very old. The color organ is really the key to it all and that goes way back. I remember seeing such a demonstration in 1928."

Continuing his discussion of color abstractions, Disney wrote, "Cy Young did something on this before he came to us—which was in 1935 or 1936. I remember him showing me stuff set to Mendelssohn's *Spring Song*."

Disney put Cy Young in charge of his Effects Department, and when it was decided to include an abstract film in the Concert Feature, as *Fantasia* was then called, naturally he put Young in charge of the project.

"Sometime in 1937 or 1938, we happened to see a reel of film by a fellow named Oskar Fischinger, a German, who was brought to our attention by an agent . . . who wanted to get him a job.

"I had a talk with the fellow and although I wasn't too impressed with him personally, when I saw his abstractions in color set to certain music, I got the idea of having him work on the Concert Feature, and gave him the job. He was employed by us from November 28, 1938, to October 31, 1939. Because of his previous experience with abstractions, he worked on *Toccata and Fugue* throughout his period of employment."

It was Oskar Fischinger who pioneered the animation of abstract lines and shapes to music that became the film form used in the opening number of *Fantasia*. In Germany, in his Study no. 8, in 1931, he used the first half of Dukas's *The Sorcerer's Apprentice*— though Fischinger made no attempt to tell the story of the magician's helper in his abstract film. Two years before Len Lye, in 1933, Fischinger had made the first color-on-film movie in Europe, *Kreise (Circles)*. Paramount Pictures offered Fischinger a contract, and he came to the United States in February, 1936.

But Fischinger, like Disney, was used to having total control over his films. Fischinger's color animation of a symphonic episode called "Radio Dynamics" was planned for *The Big Broadcast of 1937* (1936), and would have been the first abstract sequence in a commercial feature, but Fischinger brought it in overtime, over-budget, and in color. The feature was in black-and-white, and that's the way Paramount wanted its abstract sequence. The sequence was not used in the film, and Fischinger left Paramount after six months.

Leopold Stokowski conducted his orchestral arrangement of Bach's *Fugue in G Minor* in *The Big Broadcast of 1937*, and, according to William Moritz in *The Films of Oskar Fischinger*, Fischin-

*Walt's daughter, Diane, recalls that when he was working on the Bach sequence, he and Stokowski "would sit together saturating themselves in music. Father would say, 'Listen to that passage. In my mind I can see the ends of a bunch of violin bows going up and down.'" Cy Young animated cloud formations with violin bows dissolving in and out, and made the bow animation build and recede as strings and bows were introduced from the foreground into the distance. In addition, the call and answer in the music called forth color changes on the screen.*

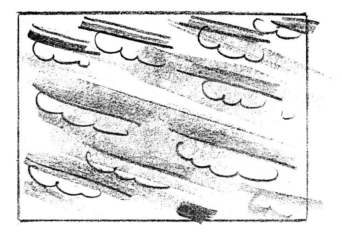

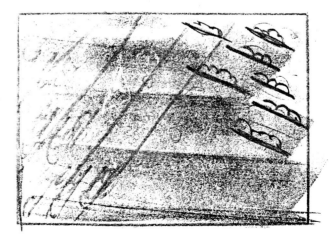

*Disney thought about color more than ever before. Listening with Stokowski to a recording of Bach's* Toccata and Fugue in D Minor *rising to a crescendo, Disney said: "That's like coming out of a dark tunnel into a glare of light." He filled* Fantasia *with experiments in sound and color consonance, as in these shots of the orchestra beginning to play: Stokowski in silhouette atop his podium, with the colored shadows of nine violinists on the screen in front of him; horn players in silhouette with rim-lighted instruments, and the tympani in blue shadows on the wall; and three French horn players in silhouette, with their horns lighting up in various colors as they play (opposite).*

ger spoke to Stokowski about making a film based on the conductor's orchestral arrangement of Bach's *Toccata and Fugue in D Minor.* Stokowski, says Moritz, "would not sign over the rights to his arrangement, without being sure that there was adequate financial backing to produce the film properly."

So how did the *Toccata and Fugue* get into *Fantasia?* According to the story meeting transcripts, Disney and Stokowski and their associates listened to a record of the composition in the Disney Studio conference room on Saturday morning, September 10, 1938, nearly three months before Fischinger joined the staff. In their search for compositions to use in *Fantasia,* they listened to hundreds of recordings. Disney had an idea for a segment about a witches' tale, and hearing *Toccata and Fugue,* he said: "I'm looking for a place to use the devil who is supposed to play the violin."

"I believe that is too straight for our purposes," said Stokowski, and recommended instead that "*Night on Bald Mountain* would be good for a witches' tale."

Walt bought that idea of Stokowski's, but he did not forget about *Toccata and Fugue.* For the story meeting held nineteen days later, a five-page summary of twelve "compositions contemplated for our musical feature" was circulated among the artists and musicians in attendance. It showed that Disney had decided to do a witches' revel to *Night on Bald Mountain* and an abstract film to the *Toccata and Fugue.*

"To abstract and mathematical music of grandeur," read the summary, "we give an abstract interpretation—abstractions, geometrical and color patterns. A fugue is the weaving together of several themes, and this has given Walt the idea for a very novel effect. All about the theaters will be concealed loud speakers. Thus, for example, we can get the effect of the music marching about the theater, coming from the ceiling, one theme moving in one direction, a second theme circling the theater in the opposite direction, all meeting at the back of the theater and marching down the aisle in unison. We are also considering third dimensional effects for this number."

Disney's idea to include 3-D glasses with cardboard frames in the *Fantasia* program and make the *Toccata and Fugue* the first commercial 3-D film (twelve years before *Bwana Devil*) was later abandoned, but experiments on Fantasound were already underway, and *Fantasia* did become the birthplace of the first stereophonic sound system in motion pictures.

On September 3, Walt told Bill Garity, his sound recording expert, that he and Stokowski wanted a unique system of speakers that would surround the audience with sound. Fantasound had its first test on September 28, the day before the *Toccata* was listed among the selections being proposed for *Fantasia.* Garity set up a test system on the sound stage and demonstrated it for Disney and Stokowski. "The circular speaker control . . . consisted of a continuously rotated fader maintaining constant output level from four loud speakers placed in the corners of the stage," wrote Garity. "The illusion is very effective and can produce a degree of dizziness on the part of the listener."

Disney's fascination with the sound track was finding its visual equivalent in the *Toccata and Fugue*. On November 8, 1938, Cy Young displayed color sketches picturing designs derived from sound tracks, progressing into rhythmic or movement patterns of pseudo-sound track design, then into fantastic designs with no relation to the sound track.

"What does the *Toccata and Fugue* represent?" Disney asked Stokowski as he studied Young's sketches.

"It is a motif or decorative pattern which gradually develops more and more," Stokowski said, "just as you have done here with the designs of the sound track. Finally, it becomes perfectly free. The theme which comes at the beginning develops more and more, with more and more voices and instruments. It is a growth like a tree growing from a seed."

"Don't you think that the last thing Cy has there is too complicated?" asked Walt, indicating some of Young's color sketches. And a few moments later he was discoursing on what he wanted their abstract film to be:

"I would like to see you stick to the sound track all the way through. We don't want to follow what anyone else has done in the abstract. We have never dealt in the abstract; we have given things a reason for existing, and tried to convince the audience that it could happen, or was possible. I think, even in this, if we take the sound track and use that and build through on that, it furnishes a reason for what we are doing on the screen."

Throughout the making of *Fantasia*, Walt would insist on these three qualities: clarity, simplification, and a reason for everything done on the screen.

Walt's idea for using 3-D to make the form of the music clearer (he had seen an experiment using glasses to achieve the illusion) excited Ed Plumb, the Studio musician who was *Fantasia's* musical director.

"It would be good if we could indicate the third dimension on the *Toccata,* then start on a plane surface on the *Fugue* and come back into the third dimension," said Plumb.

"It would be true to the *Fugue,*" replied Stokowski, "if when the theme first comes on you show a certain plane of distance, then when the second theme comes in, show a nearer plane, then nearer and still nearer, as they come in. That is what the *Fugue* does."

So while artists at the other cartoon studios were planning further adventures for Popeye and Porky Pig, artists at the Disney Studio listened to Leopold Stokowski explain form in music:

"Looking at this composition broadly," he said, "the *Toccata* is 'A,' the *Fugue* is 'B,' and we return to 'A' at the end. The *Toccata* starts off with three phrases, which are like the playing of immense trumpets to call you to attention. For that reason, this composition is a wonderful selection with which to begin your picture. It is very arresting. After that, the music goes down low and swells up to a tremendous climax at the end of the *Toccata*. The *Toccata* is really all in one mass, very much alike. Then follows the immense contrast—the *Fugue*."

But now Stokowski was "seeing" the music in his imagination, and thinking of the silence after the three phrases he asked Walt a key question:

"How will we represent the silence on the screen?"

And Walt, who was "hearing" the pictures, answered:

"At first, it will be all dark. Then the light comes up and highlights Stokowski's features. It is still dark, but as the orchestra starts, the color surges in. Stokowski becomes more of a silhouette, but still with the reflection of the color highlighting his face. Then let it all recede. In the silent spaces, we have nothing but the highlight. When the music comes in again, the color will surge up behind.

"We will tie everything together at the start, Stokowski and the orchestra, then go off into the abstract forms in the *Fugue*, then come back and mix the two at the end, then come back to the or-

A watercolor storyboard (opposite) shows Disney artists the importance of change of color in dramatizing the Bach Toccata and Fugue. The three frames from the film on this page demonstrate how color was used to enhance the shots of Leopold Stokowski conducting.

chestra. We can get the effect of depth without going into cubes, etc. We can build mountains with our sound track, going back into the distance there — like building a line of hills, then another in back of that. . . ."

At a later time Disney said, "Our definite aim, as I see it, is the sound track. I don't see blending clouds into it, or anything like that. Bach had nothing definite in mind when he composed this music—he was just dealing with music."

John Hubley, who laid out several sequences in *Rite of Spring,* once observed that he was always amazed at how easily Walt Disney could give up an idea if he felt that he had come across a better one.

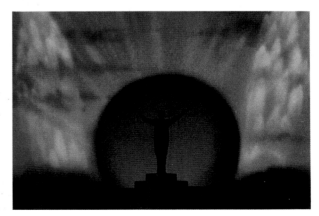

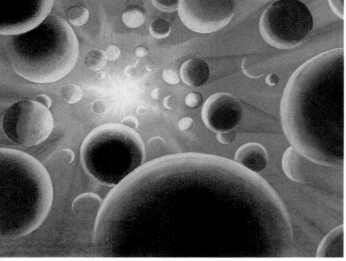

*Five abstractions made as visual accompaniment for Bach's* Toccata and Fugue. *The heavy wave action (opposite, above), with a highlight on the water to interpret the violin theme, was a simplified version of a graphic idea contributed by Oskar Fischinger, who pioneered the animation of abstract lines and shapes to music in films he made in Germany in the early 1930s. "Because of his previous experience with abstractions," wrote Disney, "he worked on* Toccata and Fugue.*" The frame (opposite, below) introduces the connection between podiums and mountaintops that runs as a motif through the picture—a revealing expression of the messianic aspirations of both Disney and Stokowski.*

"After one or two meetings, it was decided to get away from the actual sound track animation and use designs suggested by the sound track," wrote Miles Pike, a member of the crew who created the *Toccata*'s continuity. "The idea of using silhouettes of Stokie and the orchestra was acceptable at once. It was *developed* to show a relationship between the picture and the music, not only in form and color, but in instrumentation as well. The *Fugue* didn't *develop* quite as easily," Pike explained.

"Probably the most difficult problem we had to face was the creation of abstract or semiabstract forms which could be animated and not just 'pushed' across the screen. So many things had to be considered. Did the form fit the music? Was it a picture of the sound? How did it make its entrance? Did it move vertically or horizontally? Or did it rotate or follow a wave movement? And the theme! Oh, my God! don't forget the theme! It repeats seven times throughout the *Fugue*! Should the theme have its own fixed form or should the form change with the development of the theme? All this (and heaven too!) had to be clarified so that it would make up in interest what it lacked in story or continuity."

The final storyboard continuity was worked out by a team headed by Cy Young. The idea, taken from Disney, was that they were to imagine themselves sitting in a concert hall, listening to the music with their eyes closed. "What you'll see on the screen," said Deems Taylor in his introduction, "is a picture of the various abstract images that might pass through your mind. . . . At first, you are more or less conscious of the orchestra, so our picture opens with a series of impressions of the conductor and the players. Then they begin to suggest other things to your imagination. They might be—oh, just masses of color. They may be cloud forms, or vague landscapes, or vague shadows, or—geometrical objects, floating in space."

Interestingly, when Disney picked the *Toccata and Fugue* to open the *Fantasia* program instead of an overture as originally planned, his choice met strong objections from Taylor, who said: "There you are doing the only not strictly legitimate thing in the whole program. It would not be played in a symphony [concert] to open the evening. Nor a pop concert."

"But, Deems," said Stokowski, "I don't think that's a good reason. This isn't a pop concert. You can't compare this with anything. Don't think in the past tense, think in the future tense."

"Doesn't the *Toccata* demonstrate an orchestra?" Walt asked the maestro.

"Very well," said Stokowski.

"Then I don't see how—I mean, why don't we use that in the beginning?" said Walt.

And they did.

In *Art and Visual Perception*, Rudolf Arnheim has written that a "surprisingly strong expression of geometrical figures in movement has been demonstrated in the more elaborate 'abstract' films of Oskar Fischinger, Norman McLaren, Walt Disney, and others." According to Moritz, "Fischinger quit the Disney Studio in disgust and despair before the *Toccata* section had even been completed."

Fischinger was obviously an artist who was not at his best working in a group—particularly a group that he did not control. For one *Toccata* sequence that Fischinger was assigned, he planned four different and simultaneous movements. Disney's passion for simplification reduced the four movements to one: alternating wave forms. And yet that heavy wave action that uses a highlight to interpret the violin theme is one of the strongest images in the film.

The unique importance of Disney's *Toccata and Fugue* is that it presented the first animation of abstract art in a commercial feature film. It was the forerunner of the still small number of commercial films that have been made for a general audience, such as Stanley Kubrick's *2001: A Space Odyssey* (1968) and Disney's own *Tron* (1982), in which there are sections (*2001*'s "Stargate Corridor" sequence, or *Tron*'s computer-generated imagery combined with music created on a Moog synthesizer) that attempt to express feeling and emotion through color and form moving in consonance with music, rather than through drama.

It is difficult, so many years after the post-World War II acceptance of Abstract Expressionism, to imagine the resistance of the general public to abstract art before the war. Disney hoped that the novelty of wide-screen, 3-D, and stereophonic sound would win acceptance for his abstract film as the novelty of sound had finally won a place for his third Mickey Mouse cartoon in the theaters and the novelty of color had helped gain acceptance of his Silly Symphonies. Although wide-screen and 3-D proved economically unfeasible in 1940, abstract shapes moving in consonance with directional sound was apparently a success, at least according to the report of Emily Genauer, art critic of the old New York *World-Telegram*:

"We have no need to talk again of the substance of abstract art," she wrote, "to point out the beauty of form and color per se, to insist that in arbitrary improvisations of lines, shapes and spots there can be, if conceived by a true artist, as much beauty as exists in a painting of such natural forms as a landscape or a nude body. Now, we write of 'rhythmic' design, of patterns and tones arranged in counterpoint, of the delicate and exquisite relationships that can be established between planes, of plastic 'movement'—and hope to heaven we're making ourselves understood.

"Along comes Disney with his visual accompaniment to the Bach *Toccata and Fugue*—the first number in *Fantasia*—and it's all miraculously clear. . . . The whole thing is a succession of beautifully colored abstractions, with sometimes faintly discernible in them the suggestion of violin bows or the strings of a cello or the curve of a bass viol. One or two of them recall Kandinsky especially. There were several closely related to the surrealist Miró. And the opening night audience—many of whom, doubtless, raise up their hands in horror at abstract paintings—loved it."

So: did Disney and Stokowski enable us to "SEE the music and HEAR the picture"? Well, some of us did. Some of us felt the way Otis Ferguson did. He wrote of *Fantasia* that "the screen itself, when the music is playing, is the only excuse I have ever seen for having eyes and ears at the same time."

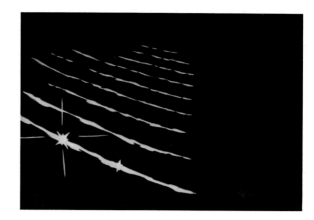

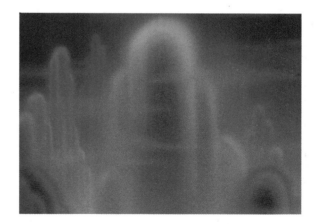

# THE NUTCRACKER

*Thistles and orchids in a spirited performance of the Russian Dance.*

# SUITE

The Nutcracker Suite consists of eight short movements taken from the music of a full-length ballet, *The Nutcracker,* by Piotr Ilyich Tchaikovsky, composed for the St. Petersburg Opera House, where it was first performed in December, 1892.

*Fantasia* uses only the last six movements of the suite, uniting them in a nature ballet danced by flowers and plants, fairies and marine creatures, through the changing seasons, from high summer through fall and finally to winter. The suite begins early in the morning with *Dance of the Sugar Plum Fairy,* performed by Dewdrop Fairies who flit over flowers, touching them with their wands and spangling them with dew. *Chinese Dance* comes to life with Hop Low and the mushroom dancers. They shake themselves vigorously, throwing off the dew, then go into their dance. The mushrooms resemble Chinese men with long robes, coolie hats, and pigtails. The smallest mushroom, Hop Low, has difficulty keeping up with the routines, and finally loses his place in the dance—but hops back in time to take a bow. In *Dance of the Reed Flutes,* blossoms drift down upon the surface of a stream. As they touch the water their petals spread out, then slowly curve upward. With inverted petals, they resemble dancers in long, swirling skirts. *Arab Dance* takes us underwater, where an undulating forest of water plants becomes a harem and goldfish resemble languid odalisques. *Russian Dance* is smartly executed by thistles who look like booted Cossacks with tall hats and fierce mustaches, and orchids who look like slim-waisted peasant girls in quaint headdresses and full skirts. *Waltz of the Flowers,* the final movement, is divided into four dances, which illustrate the change of the season. In the first, the leaves change color when Autumn Fairies touch them. In the second, when the Autumn Fairies touch milkweed pods, out float silky milkweed seeds, resembling classical ballerinas in white bouffant skirts, their black hair smooth and sleek. The third dance features the Frost Fairies, whose touch decorates nature with minute needles of blue-white ice. As they skate across the pond, its surface freezes, and they leave patterns on the glittering ice. Then Snowflake Fairies dance down, skirts whirling to the finale of the waltz.

The Chinese Dance was originally planned for oriental lizards with the Chinese mushrooms playing a minor role as lamplighters (below). Then Walt thrust the mushrooms into center stage (opposite).

"The principal object of any of the fine arts is to arouse a purely emotional reaction in the beholder," said Walt Disney when he introduced *The Story of the Animated Drawing* on his "Disneyland" television show for November 30, 1955. "The example here . . . is *The Nutcracker Suite* from *Fantasia*. This type of cartoon did not rely upon telling a story, but rather it attempted to create an emotional response in the audience by using form and color in motion to interpret fine music."

That was Walt speaking in his Tom Sawyer mode. The Huck Finn in him said the same thing in conversation this way: "If I can't feel a theme, I can't make a film that anyone else will feel. I can't laugh at intellectual humor. I'm just corny enough to like to have a story hit me over the heart."

The story of how mushrooms got into the *Chinese Dance* in *The Nutcracker Suite* is a fine example of Walt Disney's taste in entertainment. The laughter and applause of audiences suggest that it is the most successful of all the moments in *Fantasia* at evoking the most frequent reaction to the film—the emotion of delight. Yet the story conference notes show that if Walt hadn't paid his characteristic attention to detail, the mushroom dance might well have lost out to some Chinese lizards.

At the beginning of the Concert Feature story exploration under Dick Huemer in the old apartment house at Hyperion, a storyman named Jerry Brewer was assigned to continuity development of *The Nutcracker Suite* with an extensive crew.

As overall story director, Huemer would visit the crew every day to see what they'd done, if it seemed to be working, if it was ready to show to Walt. Huemer remembered this part as particular fun because three imaginative women were making sketches for the storyboard—Sylvia Moberly-Holland, Bianca Majolie, and Ethel Kulsar. They would pick weeds in vacant lots near the Studio and bring them in and draw them up as dancers in *The Nutcracker Suite*'s ballet of nature. A mass of common thistles, for example, suggested an energetic band of Cossacks, complete with belted blouses, tall hats, and boots. From there it was a short step to seeing clusters of orchids as lovely peasant girls in quaint headdresses and full skirts. And there you had the cast for the *Russian Dance*.

At this time, the Disney Studio had a Camera Club, whose monthly shows were given critiques by celebrated local photogaphers. Hidden away in a Studio news release on the club is the information that "one of the Disney Camera Club members had the private sideline of photographing flowers and mushrooms, prints of which he kept mounted in a book at the studio. During early research on *The Nutcracker Suite* . . . the sequence director saw this book, recognized that many mushrooms have an oriental look. . . ."

The sequence director of *The Nutcracker Suite* was Sam Armstrong, the background artist on *Snow White* who painted the memorable watercolor of the Seven Dwarfs' cottage as the princess first sees it. Armstrong apparently asked a character designer named John Walbridge to make some drawings of mushrooms that look like Chinese, and Walbridge used the radial structure of the plant to suggest coolie hats and eyes with epicanthic folds. Brewer assigned these characters a minor role in the *Chinese Dance* as lamplighters lighting up dewdrops, and Walbridge did another model sheet full of mushroom drawings (confusing his fungi, he called them "Chinese Toadstool Dancers"). In these drawings he made their stocky bodies suggest people in tight robes that reached down to the ground and that permitted locomotion only through small steps.

Nevertheless, Jerry Brewer made no mention of mushrooms when he wrote his brief synopsis of the visual accompaniment planned for *The Nutcracker Suite* on November 1, 1938.

"This is to be a typical oriental dance," wrote Brewer of the *Chinese Dance.* "Chinese, Japanese, Javanese, or Siamese, in which one male dancer with high decorative headdress, short, tight skirt and curled toed shoes executes an authentic dance before a background of swaying oriental girls. The entire dance is staged for a frog mandarin."

Three weeks later Brewer spread out the rough continuity sketches and explained what he envisioned to Disney. For more than a year, Walt had been following the gradual development of the sequence, which now had oriental lizards dancing for a frog mandarin, and he was not satisfied.

"I don't know, Jerry," said Walt. "Here's what I see. There's something very valuable in these little mushrooms that look like Chinese characters. That in itself is valuable, and you want to have a chance to see them, and see what they do."

Toward the end of the meeting, after several other sections of the *Nutcracker* had been discussed, Walt went back to the character model drawings of the Chinese mushrooms that were dated November 4, 1938.

"I like these models," said Walt. "I don't think we can improve much on them. They're the result of a hell of a lot of work. Johnny worked on them a year or so ago, then came back with these new ones that I think are very good. The poppies are ideal for the Chinese things, and the mushrooms look swell for the little coolies."

At the end of the meeting, Disney cautioned Brewer against much elaboration of the lizards-frog mandarin approach to the *Chinese Dance.* "Jerry," he said, "I think you can work on this from the angle that you don't go into such elaborate sketches until we arrive at what we're going to do. I think we'll get farther with it now — we've got a certain line on it. Just work on it and keep it simple, and we can get together on it in about a week."

Reading between the lines of the story conference notes, one can see that the models of the mushrooms as Chinese coolies had hit Walt over the heart.

The *Chinese Dance* was performed — according to the program — by "Hop Low and the Mushroom Dancers." This brief sequence is one of the highest points that the animated film has yet reached. Hop Low, the littlest mushroom, projects his personality as vividly as any character in the Disney galaxy — yet he has no dialogue, makes no sound, and doesn't even have a face or hands to gesture with. He is the best example of the Disney Studio's genius for compression, its ability to spring an entire character from a simple design in motion. Indeed, the only three artists that Walt Disney credited with the *Nutcracker Suite* character designs are John Walbridge, Elmer Plummer (who drew the mushrooms in color), and Ethel Kulsar, who designed the Russian thistles.

Normally the sequence director would take over from the Story Department when the story was finished. In this case, Sam Armstrong took over from Jerry Brewer while the story was still being developed. He and Walt threw out the idea of using the mushrooms as lamplighters lighting the dewdrops and made them the only performers of the *Chinese Dance.* After that, the idea of contrasting a little mushroom with big mushrooms grew out of the music (and Walbridge's November 4 model sheet, which showed a big mushroom juggling three little mushrooms).

"In the *Chinese Dance,*" said a storyman identified in the notes only as "R," "you have an antithesis, a contrast between the brilliant piccolos and the pizzicato strings. That should be brought out more on the screen, so the same design doesn't go through these two. If you have the same decoration on the screen with the two contrasting parts of the music, it doesn't go together, it seems to me." The criticism bore fruit.

An artist identified in the notes as "P" suggested that it might be small mushrooms and large mushrooms.

"Yes, that would be it exactly," said R — and when the small mushrooms were simplified to be one small mushroom, Hop Low was born.

Considering how little the animator had to work with, it was likely that the *Chinese Dance* would have been animated without "the little fellow" emerging as a personality on the screen. If you want to see how likely, watch the broom come to life and go through

*Hop Low hops—in 14 drawings by Art Babbitt. The inspirational sketch for the Chinese Dance (above) now had mushrooms instead of lizards, but it didn't yet have the littlest mushroom, Hop Low, who would steal the show.*

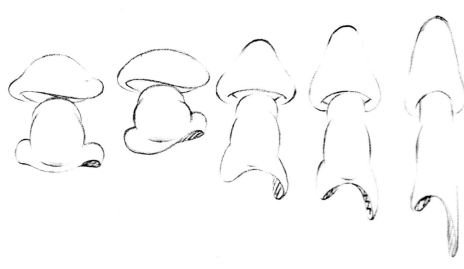

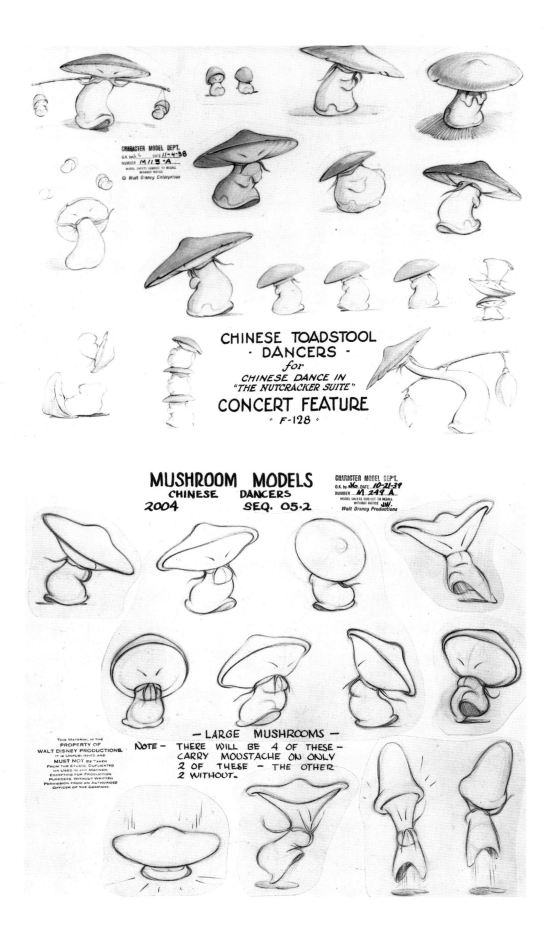

CHINESE TOADSTOOL
- DANCERS -
for
CHINESE DANCE IN
"THE NUTCRACKER SUITE"
CONCERT FEATURE
" F-128 "

MUSHROOM MODELS
CHINESE DANCERS
2004                    SEQ. 05-2

- LARGE MUSHROOMS -
NOTE - THERE WILL BE 4 OF THESE -
CARRY MOUSTACHE ON ONLY
2 OF THESE - THE OTHER
2 WITHOUT.

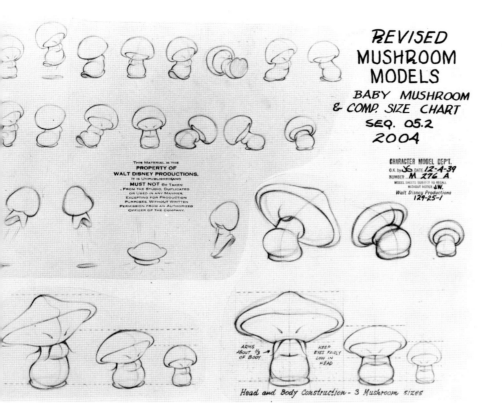

The evolution of the Chinese mushrooms can be traced through these model sheets and storyboard sketch. On November 4, 1938 (opposite, above), when Fantasia was still called Concert Feature, they were called "Chinese toadstool dancers." They were identified as "mushrooms" on the model sheet of October 21, 1939 (opposite, below), but the babies who had been juggled and carried in the earlier model sheet were absent. The "Revised Mushroom Models" of December 4, 1939, however, establishes the comparative sizes of the three mushroom models (left), and the smallest mushroom is clearly the star of the story sketch (below). It only remained for animator Art Babbitt to conceive the way that Chinese mushrooms moved.

Storyboard sketches show Hop Low about to march
toward the camera through two rows of larger
mushrooms (above), and falling out of the scene in the
Serpentine Dance. Animator Babbitt imbued the
little guy with a heart-winning cockiness that made
him move among the big boys as if he were reviewing
his troops, and get out of step as if he were the
only one in step. It is the magic of Babbitt's animation
that an anthropomorphized mushroom with no
mouth or nose—and only the barest suggestion of
eyes—could convey his attitudes so clearly.

his paces in *The Sorcerer's Apprentice* without developing a memorable personality. The animator who put the spark of personality into Hop Low was Arthur Babbitt.

When Art Babbitt was asked what he thought made the dancing mushrooms work so well, he answered:

"An element of warmth was injected. A little story was told. It was the story of one character who was constantly out of step with all the others, and he never did quite get into the crowd. Except there was one occasion — I think it was the scene where he marches toward the camera and then on back as if he were reviewing his troops — which gives you an indication of the little guy's cocky character. In spite of the fact that almost everything he does is wrong, it's full of mistakes, he does have his one moment of glory when he does it just right. He is not aware — or he refuses to accept — that he is at fault; that there is something wrong with him."

"Now, how did he develop and dance his way out of the chorus?" Babbitt was asked.

"He developed in many ways," said Babbitt. "For instance, the anticipation for his steps at the beginning of the dance is almost a direct swipe — although you may never have recognized it — from these three zanys who keep slapping each other all around — the Three Stooges. One of the Three Stooges always did a funny little action where the knees overlap. When he would get angry he would do this little furious step, with his knees crossing, one over the other. And instead of just an ordinary anticipation, I used this, because the music called for a trill. So during that trill, he did this little anticipatory act.

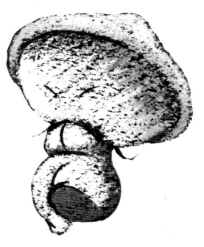

"Also, the music dictated certain things. I don't know a hell of a lot about music, but there is a phrase that is stated once: there's a statement. Then I think it's repeated, the same phrase. Then there's an answer, I don't remember if it's repeated once or twice. And then they come back to the original line of music. So that gave me the architecture."

Babbitt remembered the color models of the mushrooms drawn by Elmer Plummer — mushrooms as the personifications of a small group of Chinese, dressed in long robes and wearing coolie hats, with just a suggestion of pigtail underneath. "Plummer's drawings were very nice," he said. "But as you work with them, and endow them with life — as they start to animate, certain changes take place. So the animation changed the designs slightly from Plummer's drawings, and then there were other changes that took place when Bill Hurtz, Babbitt's assistant, cleaned up my drawings. And then there were enhancing things that were added by the Effects Department." The sequence begins with mushrooms vigorously throwing off the morning dew, and Babbitt praised the effects artists who created "little drops of dew glistening."

To work out the choreography, Babbitt drew with a music score pinned to his desk, so that he could relate the action not only to the melodic line, but also to the counterpoint — "those nasty little notes underneath." For instance, in the *Chinese Dance*, Babbitt explains, "there's a bass underneath. So something has to be related to that, too. So, as I played the music over and over again, and studied the sheet, I began to 'see' what is happening. I can actually see it. When you have 'Buh-buh-buh-buh,' that's the little guy coming forward; and then it repeats, and he goes backward."

Al Zinnen, the layout man, "planned the overall *ideal* composition," said Babbitt, "but you can't stick with that, because your characters are moving around constantly, and what might be a composition for one bit of action doesn't necessarily fit a succeeding bit of action. And your camera is not nailed down. In effect, you are the camera.

"The only choreographic suggestion I ever got came from Walt Disney himself. I had animated the little mushroom taking his bow on the last note of music. Walt suggested he take the bow after. Both ways would have worked, depending on one's translation of the little guy's character."

Art Babbitt is a camera with brains and a pulse. In the *Chinese Dance*, through a combination of perfect timing, a masterful use of space, and the ability to empathize with a little mushroom, he achieved more with less than any other animator in history. But without Disney's timely intervention, it might have been the *Dance of the Chinese Lizards*.

The *Nutcracker Suite* was the natural culmination of a decade of efforts by the Disney Studio to use the rhythm of nature as the subject of animated films. These efforts began in 1929-30 with a cycle of Silly Symphonies on the theme of the seasons (*Springtime* in 1929; *Summer, Autumn,* and *Winter* in 1930). In these cartoons, the Disney Studio gave a visual interpretation of the spirit of nature through patterns of action carefully related to snatches of such popular classics as *Dance of the Hours,* which also appears on the *Fantasia* program. In the earlier visualization of *Dance of the Hours,* frogs eat insects, birds eat frogs, in what Don Graham, head of the Disney Studio art school, called "an unwinding sequence of . . . [lively] actions, always ending in extermination. Action and music combined to create a specific atmosphere: the essence of spring and youth, with the inevitable reminder of death."

In such cartoons as *The Grasshopper and the Ants* (1934), when the winter wind blows fall colors to icy hues, Disney added change of color to movement as an expression of the rhythm of the seasons. But in all these cartoons, birds, animals, and insects did most of the dancing. As early as May, 1935, however, Disney story people began working on a much more imaginative fantasy idea in which the inanimate world of plants and flowers would join in the dance. When they first began "kicking the idea around," it was intended for a Silly Symphony to be called *Ballet des Fleurs.* By the time it went into production, it had become part of the Concert Feature and would embrace most of Tchaikovsky's *Nutcracker Suite.*

Samuel Armstrong was one of ten directors whom Disney assigned to oversee *Fantasia*'s eight sequences from the time they left the story rooms until they reached the screen. Armstrong directed *Toccata and Fugue* and *The Nutcracker Suite*; James Algar

*When Babbitt's drawings of mushrooms were inked onto transparent sheets of celluloid that were then painted on the reverse side, when Special Effects animated dewdrops over these mushroom drawings, and when Camera photographed them over a background painting of the spotlight in the darkness, the opening long shot of the* Chinese Dance *could be projected on screens all over the world. Now, as then, mushrooms in a cluster suddenly shake their heads, throwing dewdrops in all directions, jump out into a circle, and start to dance—with Hop Low in the center.*

The Dance of the Sugar Plum Fairy is performed by Dewdrop Fairies. In the frame above, a fairy hovers around morning glories that light up when she touches them with her wand and fade as she departs. The hovering action, based on the movement of the hummingbird, is seen in the animation drawings of Les Clark (opposite). For Waltz of the Flowers, Clark animated Autumn Fairies, who touched vines and leaves with their wands, turning them to autumn colors—as with the clematis leaves at right.

directed *The Sorcerer's Apprentice*; Bill Roberts and Paul Satterfield codirected *Rite of Spring* (with Roberts handling the sequences with dinosaurs); Hamilton Luske, Jim Handley, and Ford Beebe codirected *The Pastoral Symphony*; T. Hee and Norman Ferguson codirected *Dance of the Hours*; and Wilfred Jackson directed both *Night on Bald Mountain* and *Ave Maria.* Some of the units that worked under a *Fantasia* director were very large: Armstrong's unit had no fewer than fifty-three artists.

When Walt Disney made *Fantasia, The Nutcracker* was no longer in the repertoire of any ballet company and, as George Balanchine lamented, "People think of *The Nutcracker* as a suite rather than a ballet. *First* it was a ballet." (In 1954, Balanchine revived the full-length *Nutcracker* with the New York City Ballet, and it has been a Christmas sellout ever since.)

"The search for ideas was wide and varied," reported the *Fantasia* edition of the Disney Studio house organ.

No doubt remembering that the models for the Russian Cossack thistles were discovered in a vacant lot near the Studio, Disney sent Sylvia Holland (story development), Ethel Kulsar (background paintings), Curt Perkins, and Herman Schultheis to Idyllwild, a real nature preserve, in search of similar inspiration. When they came back to the Studio, they photographed the drawings they had made on what the Disney studio called a "Leica Reel." It was a device for projecting the drawings a frame at a time in synchronization with the appropriate musical passage, so that Walt could see, for example, what music fit best with orange leaves, what with red, what with clematis seeds, what with milkweed pods. It was a way to determine if the staging of a scene "felt" right with the music before spending the time and money necessary to animate the scenes. When the music reached the point where the Frost Fairies are to arrive, for example, the Leica Reel's electric eye would simply trigger the projection of a story sketch of Frost Fairies. The image either worked with the musical passage or it didn't.

Throughout *The Nutcracker Suite,* we see the conference method operating at its best, with ideas being tossed around until they suggested drawings, with the drawings in the Leica Reels changing and evolving until they clicked. One day, when Walt was attending a meeting, he suddenly said to Ed Plumb, the musical director:

"We want to cut the Overture."

"We talked of that too," said Plumb.

"You mean it's okay?" said Walt. "I expected a battle."

(Although Disney had final authority, he did allow himself to be talked out of ideas—as when, in *Bambi,* he wanted to show the charred bodies of the hunters, burned to death by the forest fire they had carelessly started. "How do you want the bodies drawn, Walt?" asked one of his artists. "Medium rare or well done?" Disney dropped the idea.)

"Now, here's what I'd like to see after the *March,* which we'll use as the Overture," said Walt. "We'll go into the *Sugar Plum Fairy.* The *March* ends with a boomp and we fade out and fade in on one of the Dewdrop Fairies, then we end that, they go out, and the lamp-

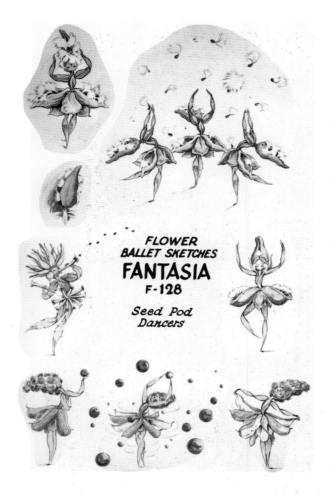

FLOWER
BALLET SKETCHES
**FANTASIA**
F-128

Seed Pod
Dancers

lighters come in and the place is full of dewdrops. Carry the dewdrops into the *Chinese Dance,* with the lamplighters, and at the end of the lamplighting sequence we find the mandarin [*sic*] there, and then the poppies blow off and come down and form those little Chinese figures that do the dance—the *Dance of the Reed Flutes* around the mandarin, and he can join in with these little figures and go back to sit on his throne. Then we can figure out an ending to that that would lead us underwater for the *Arab Dance,* with the goldfish. . . ."

In the end, the first *two* movements were omitted, and the mushrooms became the only figures in the *Chinese Dance.* "Also, the original order of the movements has been somewhat altered," wrote Deems Taylor, "on the theory that since the work *is* a suite, and not a symphony, there is no vital connection among the movements, and that the order in which they are heard, provided it be musically effective, is immaterial. In devising the animated screen pictures that go with the music, Walt Disney was confronted with the fact that if he presented the suite simply as a series of dances, with no central theme, the result would be merely a group of unrelated short subjects." Disney's solution was to envision the suite as a whole, as a ballet of nature, danced by plants and flowers, fairies, and marine creatures.

Sugar Plum Fairies did not fit in with Disney's nature ballet theme, so they were transformed into Dewdrop Fairies—sprites who decorate dandelions and spider webs with dewdrops so that they sparkle in the sunshine. (A special transparent paint was developed for this dance, adding greatly to its beauty.) Director Sam Armstrong had suggested to Walt that "the fairies can dart around like a hummingbird, then stay poised, still in the air with their wings humming; then dart again." Les Clark animated the scene in which the fairy hovers around the honeysuckle, decorating it with dewdrops; and the fairy's dart-and-hover movements did indeed result from Clark's study of rapidly fluttering hummingbirds.

In the Disney version of *Dance of the Reed Flutes,* inverted blossoms wafted by a breeze suggest ballerinas with gauzy bell-shaped skirts. That was the way Walt saw them when he looked at some flower sketches.

"Those little flowers," he said, "I see no reason why they can't dance right on the water. If you throw a flower blossom on the water it floats; they could skim right on the water; it would make a beautiful setup. . . . When those little blossoms land on the water it's almost like the wind is blowing them around; just like the little things are dancing, but really the wind is blowing them. Then in the end— that boom—they all go over something and disappear."

As it reached the screen, a white flower landed on a stream in a pattern of swirling movement that is one of the loveliest in *Fantasia.* It is carried ahead of the multicolored flowers, like a solo dancer accompanied by a colorful chorus. Cy Young, an effects animator with a feeling for the abstract, did this scene, and he also whirled the blossoms toward the camera and—boom—over a waterfall, which turned out to be the "something they all go over and disappear."

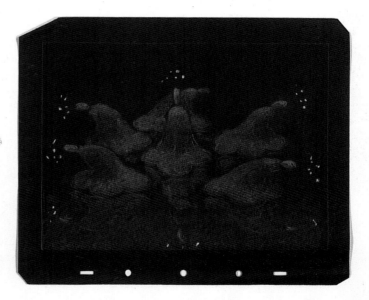

The Disney version of The Nutcracker Suite told no
story. Walt envisioned a nature ballet danced by
flowers and plants, fairies, and marine creatures: "It
should be something beautiful and something
fantastic—a will-o'-the-wisp feeling." Gradually, ideas
suggested pictures and pictures suggested movements.
Seed pod dancers (opposite) slowly evolved into the
Milkweed Ballet of Waltz of the Flowers. The pastel
drawings of blossoms dancing on the water became
the Blossom Ballet to Dance of the Reed Flutes.

The Arab Dance *became a water ballet danced by fish.* "Never has an object on celluloid looked so diaphanous and delicate," *wrote Frank Thomas and Ollie Johnston of the fish pictured above. Animator Don Lusk and his assistants drew not only the fish but all the sparkles, the effects animation, the shadings on the tails and fins that created the moment of beauty. Since each group of drawings meant another cel level for this scene that runs for 112 feet of film, the result was a stack of drawings taller than one person could carry to the Camera Department.*

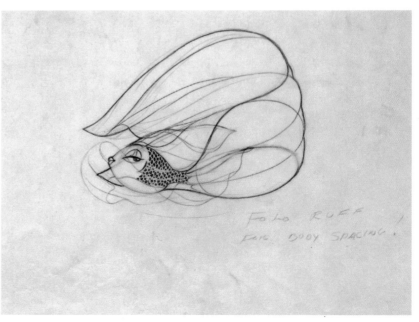

Considerable live-action film was shot for this dance, performed by two professional dancers, Joyce Coles and Marjorie Belcher. Miss Belcher had already modeled for Snow White and for the Blue Fairy in *Pinocchio.* For this dance she and Miss Coles were costumed in long tulle ballet skirts that resembled the shape of the blossoms that were to skim across the water. The difference between that live action and the animation that resulted is the difference between dancing on a stage and dancing on water.

*Arab Dance* is an *under*water ballet, performed by goldfish. Walt knew exactly what he wanted here: "There should be a regular festival—a ballet of fish—all to that slow Arabian music. All the undergrowth has a slow, wavy rhythm to the slow beats. You've seen travelogues where they take you into a harem. As you go through the courtyard, veiled ladies peek through the windows and duck back. If the cameraman wants to get a picture, they run away. Two girls peek out and see a stranger and giggle and get back to cover."

Disney's story-sketch artists gave him exactly what he wanted: goldfish peeking through undersea coral formations that suggest the latticework of the harem behind which Arab women were concealed.

Walt studied the sketches and spurred his artists on: "These fish are beautiful, lazy things—very feminine and sexy—even going further than the sketches. There is a natural hootchy-kootchy motion to a goldfish that can be made use of here."

To study that "natural hootchy-kootchy motion" in humans so that it would be available for reference by the animators, director Armstrong and storyman Norman Wright arranged to shoot live action of an Arab dancer. One day Sam Armstrong was informed by casting that Princess Omar would see him at three o'clock.

At five minutes to three Armstrong and Wright found awaiting them a swarthy-skinned Arab interpreter, a brown-eyed comely maid, and her mother. The interpreter explained the phenomenal experience of the Princess, who had danced before crowned heads. The Princess then retired to her dressing room. When she reappeared (clad mostly in her reputation) she performed something vaguely appropriate for a harem to a phonograph record. The interpreter explained that she normally carried her own Arab orchestra, but had been uncertain of Disney requirements. He asked Armstrong for his reactions. Armstrong explained that what he wanted was this—and this—and this. The interpreter turned to the Princess and, speaking in Arabic, gave quite a lot of time to explaining the Disney requirements. The Princess listened carefully, then turned to Sam Armstrong.

"Sure!" she said. "It's a cinch!"

Think of her when you see the silky, sinuous movements of the fish in *Arab Dance.*

Walt Disney had over a thousand employees at the time he was making *Fantasia;* of the fifty-three who worked on *The Nutcracker Suite,* only twenty-two received credit in the program. (There were no credits on the screen.) Some studied belly dancers and drew goldfish; others studied ballerinas and drew blossoms; one drew a little mushroom and thought of the Three Stooges. Otis Ferguson of

61

the *New Republic* was right on the mark when he said of Disney at this period, "He apparently has known how to pick his men, train them, and give them free rein to contribute their individual best. A film is a collective enterprise anyway and should be made that way; but in general there are too few men of talent at the top who have the leadership and patience, the exaltation of job over ego, to do it. Walt Disney is a pioneer in more things than his conception of and tireless experiment with the animated cartoon as a reflection of life."

For example, it was the function of a Disney director to explain to the layout artists and animators in his unit exactly what Walt wanted. As an audiovisual guide, the animator would get a phonograph record (nowadays it is a tape cassette) of the sound for his scenes, a photostat of the storyboard worked out by Walt and his Story Department, and an exposure sheet made out by the director. As explained in the first chapter, an exposure sheet is the guide to the timing of the scene. But in a sequence as subtle as the *Arab Dance,* a good animator would rely on his own sense of timing. Animators Don Lusk and Sandy Strothers had to suggest both goldfish and belly dancers at the same time. In one scene, for instance, the fish even suggests a woman wearing sheer harem pants by the quickly changing positions of its undulating fins.

Artists who would later rise to the top of their professions contributed to *The Nutcracker Suite.* John Hench, senior vice president and prime visualizer at WED, the Glendale, California, dreamtank that Walt founded to design his amusement parks, began by painting backgrounds for *The Nutcracker Suite* and later emerged as one of the Studio's top colorists on such features as *Cinderella, Alice in Wonderland,* and *Peter Pan.* Jules Engel, now head of the animation graphics department of the California Institute of the Arts, contributed a number of pastel drawings of thistles and orchids on black paper that he says inspired Sam Armstrong to stage the Chinese and Russian dances against black rather than against the naturalistic backgrounds that are the style of the rest of *The Nutcracker Suite.*

*Waltz of the Flowers* took its inspiration from a comment that Walt made at a story conference, when he said: "I'm just wondering—we've devoted a lot of our picture to flowers as they are in the summer, with their full color—and I'm just wondering if there isn't enough beauty in autumn itself. Then I think your opening would be changing from summer colors into the colors of autumn—the leaves, everything that would show a change. That harp music is swell for the color change."

In the finished film, the harp glissandos accompany the change of the leaves from pale green to yellow to orange as the Autumn Fairies move among them, touching them, turning them to the colors of autumn. When the Frost Fairies touch the leaves, the leaves encrust with frost in a virtuoso display of effects animation. The Frost Fairies freeze the water with a skating action animated by Robert Stokes, which includes a marvelous recreation of the one-two-three-step-glide of human skaters as it might be executed by fairy sprites.

*When Walt Disney fell in love with an idea, his enthusiasm was contagious. The idea of a Milkweed Ballet seemed to him an opportunity to put beauty on the screen. "If you have a pod, and the fairies touch it," he said, "all the seeds fly out almost as if they're alive . . . I think there's something beautiful in those seeds ballet-ing through the air; I like to use them because we can get off the ground and have our ballet in the air . . . they blow through the wind— they have regular ballet formations like those little girls with the long skirts. It's like ballet dancers against space." Such word pictures prompted his artists to produce the paintings of the possibilities that we see on the opposite page.*

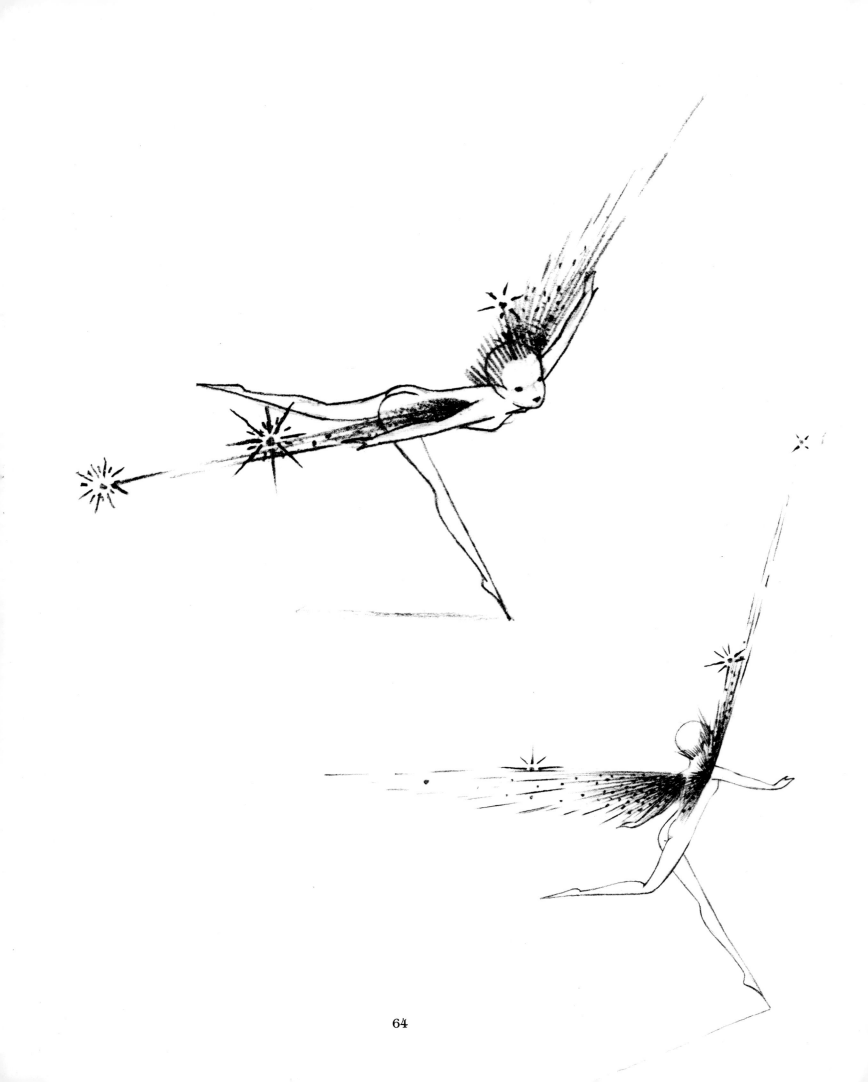

Frost Fairies in skating action called forth a powerful delicacy from Robert Stokes, whose line drawings captured the speed and grace of these inspirational sketches.

When the leaves are touched by the Frost Fairies, they encrust with frost in a virtuoso display of effects animation. The frame from the film (below) shows that rare achievement: a scene that gets most of the pictorial beauty of the inspirational sketches (opposite and above) onto the screen. This was accomplished by the most elaborate cel work ever attempted. After pencil drawings were traced onto the cels in colored ink, the cels were enhanced by drybrush, stipple, airbrush for milkweed puffs, and—for the Dewdrop Fairies—transparent paint to give the effect of a scene lighted with incandescent dewdrops.

The original models for these Russian Cossack thistles were found growing in a parking lot near the Studio. "Here are these little thistles standing there looking at you," Walt told a story meeting on November 25, 1938, "and as the music starts they go into the 'Russian Dance.'. . . How would it be if they jumped at you? You come in on this setting . . . and they're waiting there—then 'HEY!' and they jump up at you— that's definitely comic."

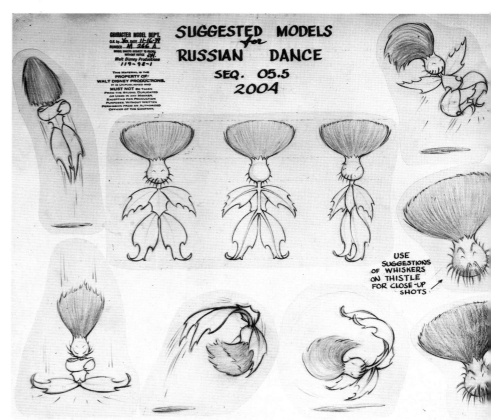

Of all things of beauty in *Fantasia*, the *Milkweed Ballet* is the most poignantly lovely. Autumn Fairies touch milkweed pods and milkweed ballerinas emerge and are airborne. It is late in the season, and their dance is brief.

"If you have a pod, and the fairies touch it," Walt told a story meeting, "all the seeds fly out almost as if they're alive. Actually, the wind does it, but you get the illusion they're alive. . . . I think there's something beautiful in those seeds ballet-ing through the air; I like to use them because we can get off the ground and have our ballet in the air."

These abstractions of dancers whose milky-colored puffs resemble white tulle skirts, whose dark seeds gleam like the slick black hair of Ludmilla Tcherina dancing *Les Sylphides* in *The Red Shoes,* float to earth like parachutes against a deep blue background while autumn leaves whirl through their scenes on gusts of wind. The composition of these scenes (Bruce Bushman and Robert Cormack did the layouts; Brad Case and George Rowley the animation) is very fine. The eye can follow the movements of a large number of milkweed ballerinas because they form a harmonious pattern within the central field of vision.

At the climax, snow begins to fall. Small Snowflake Fairies come from a distance toward the camera, filling the air with eddying, sparkling crystals, beautifully timed in their movements by George Rowley. At the end, snow covers the landscape.

Those skirts of snowflake crystals whirling down from the heavens made a moving image that Walt was determined to put on the screen. He had tried to get it into the coming of winter in *Bambi,* but it was too fanciful; he saw it again while listening to Rachmaninoff's *Troika,* then rejected *Troika* for *Fantasia*; now, finally, when the *Waltz of the Flowers* was changed to portray autumn and the coming of winter, the trait he called his "stick-to-it-ivity" found a place for them.

"One of the most arduous tasks in developing an overall style for *The Nutcracker*," said the Disney Studio house organ, "was getting away from the ten-acre lot type of staging, and finally achieving a tiny and intimate world as a stage. In this gnat's eye view of things was fantasy finally found."

It was found, in fact, in the quality that gives Walt Disney's imagination its enduring charm. "It is the charm," wrote Otis Ferguson in 1934, "of an imagination that can perceive all sorts of fantastic attitudes and action in things so common, so near to anyone's hand, that the sudden contrast of what they might be with what they certainly are not is universally droll, and not to be resisted." And so, mushrooms are contrasted with Chinese dancers, thistles with Russian dancers, and goldfish with Arab dancers; a white blossom is imagined to be a prima ballerina, and a breeze becomes her music.

Dance critic Walter Terry wrote: "Dance lovers will find much of *Fantasia* rewarding in its choreographic scope, stimulating in its brilliant use of a great art . . . bringing great dance and simple dance to everyone." This is nowhere truer than in *The Nutcracker Suite,* where animated fantasy finds a *corps de ballet* in a milkweed pod.

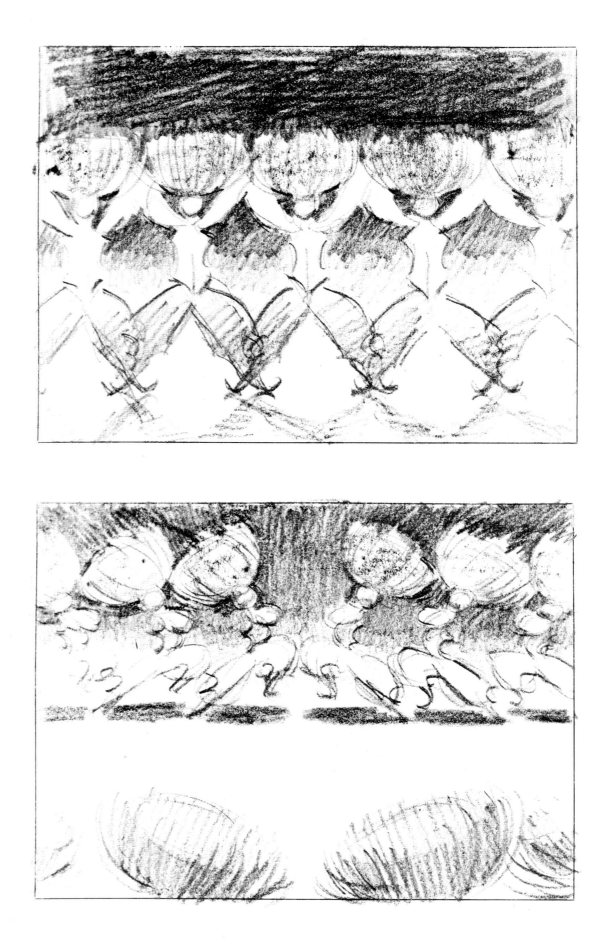

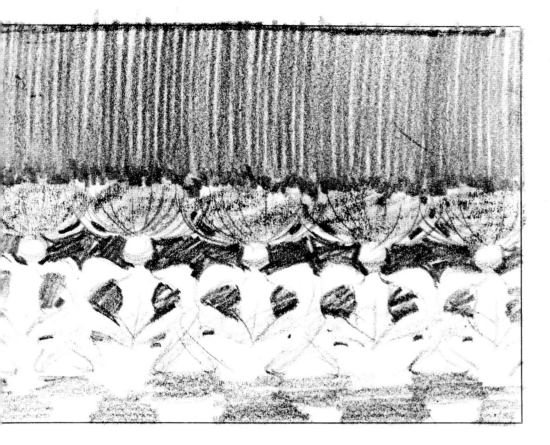

Story sketches show that from the beginning the artists were thinking of the Russian Dance in terms of patterns of movement and not in terms of individual dancers, as in the Chinese or Arab dances.

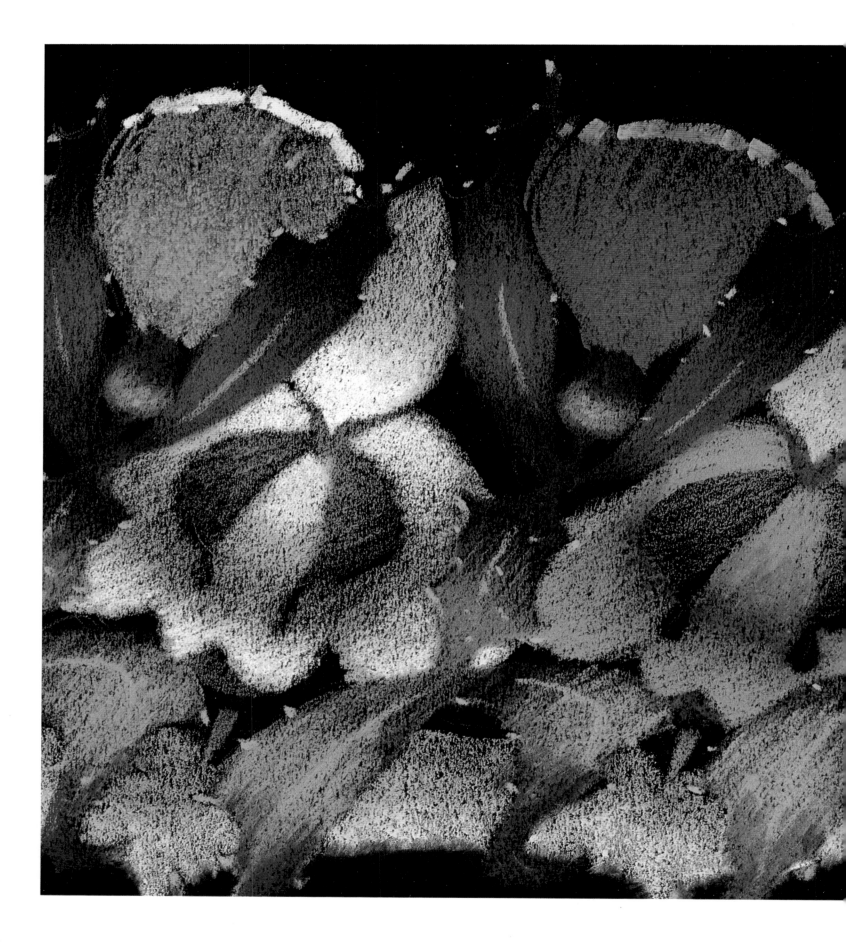

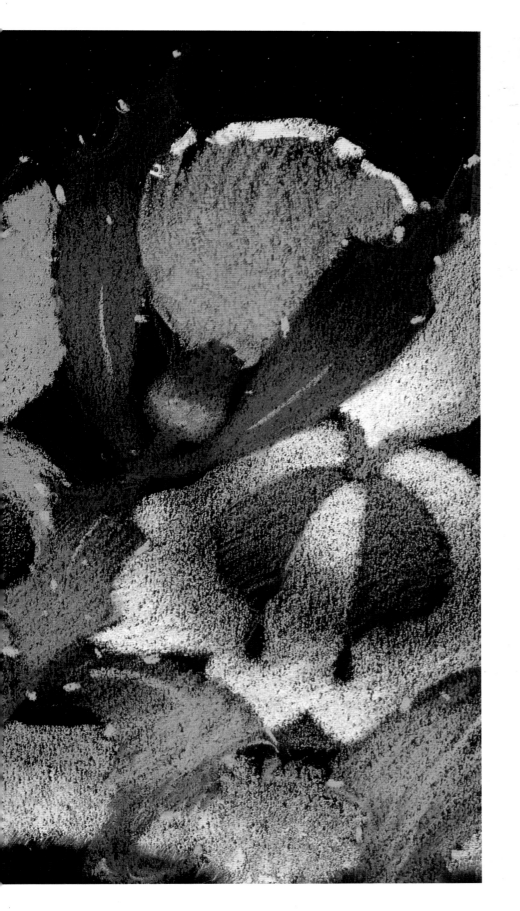

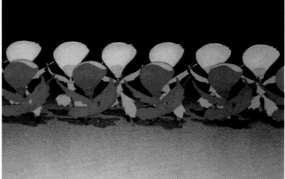

Harvard professor Robert D. Feild, in his 1942 study
The Art of Walt Disney, *pointed out that the
cooperation between Disney's Character Model
Department and his Story Department was so close
"that model sketches are frequently pinned on
the story-boards, taking their places naturally to
indicate new lines of thought. The sketches are made
in any medium, but generally in color, not with
any idea that the color used will be final but because
the artist is trying to visualize the character in
as complete a way as possible." But there were times
when the model sketches' color scheme reached
the screen, as in the case of the inspirational painting
(left) of thistles with red and yellow heads dancing
toward the camera, and the actual frame (above).*

Exploring the visual possibilities of the Russian
Dance, Disney artists contrasted the Thistle Men with
Orchid Women in various colors (opposite), and saw
them dancing in various settings, whirling like
dervishes—and even being approached by a luminous
Dewdrop Fairy (above). A simple, black-and-white
story sketch in pencil (opposite, below), suggested the
full-color tableau of thistles in repose that ended the
sequence.

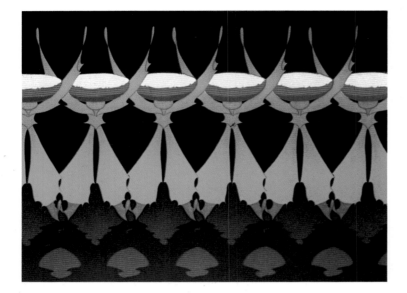
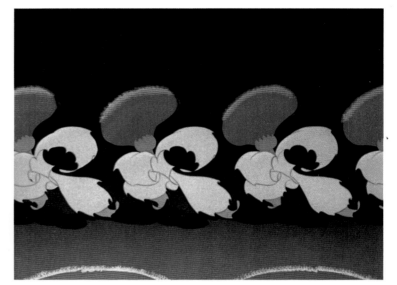

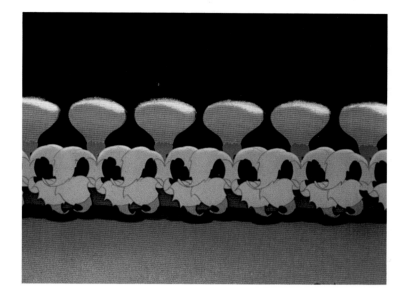

Sam Armstrong's direction, Al Zinnen's layouts, and Art Babbitt's impeccable sense of design in motion combined to create Fantasia's most successful non-objective sequence. As a color abstraction of a folk dance involving Cossacks and peasant girls, this animation of shapes suggesting both thistles and orchids and men and women was a triumph of the imagination.

A phalanx of living brooms with looming shadows makes an overwhelming bucket brigade.

# APPRENTICE

**T**he *Sorcerer's Apprentice*, a scherzo for orchestra by Paul Dukas, was first performed in Paris in 1897. Like *Fantasia* itself, the composition is a translation of one medium into another, a humorous retelling in music of Goethe's ballad *Der Zauberlehrling (The Apprentice Magician)*, about a magician's lazy apprentice who, while his master is away, uses the incantations he has learned to bring a broom to life and make it carry water for him. The film begins with the Sorcerer conjuring up a bat and changing it into a butterfly as his apprentice, Mickey Mouse, weary from carrying water, wipes his brow. Bored with his own tricks, the Sorcerer yawns, removes his tall pointed hat, and leaves his cavern.

As soon as he is alone, Mickey puts on the Sorcerer's hat and commands his broom to come to life, pick up the buckets, and carry water for him from the fountain outside to the huge vat in the cavern. Once he has the broom settled into this routine, Mickey falls asleep in an armchair and dreams that he is standing high on a cliff, conducting the clouds and stars and planets in their courses, and calling up waves from the sea below. When the waves crash over him, Mickey awakes in alarm to find that the armchair is floating in water that fills the cavern.

Mickey commands the broom to stop—but the broom walks right over him on its way to the fountain for more water. Mickey grabs an ax and chops the broom into splinters. Each splinter comes to life as a new broom. Each new broom carries two more buckets. This broom army marches inexorably to the fountain, fills all its buckets, then lines up to pour a flood of water into the cavern. Mickey's efforts to bail out the cavern are completely futile. Frantically, he climbs onto the Sorcerer's huge magic book, which is riding the whirlpool, and searches for a formula to stop the brooms. No luck. At this moment, the Sorcerer returns, parting the waters as he descends the stairs. He commands the flood to vanish and the broom army to become one broom again. Then he contemplates the apprentice who did all this mischief. Chastened, Mickey takes off the Sorcerer's hat and returns it to his unsmiling master. He hands the broom to the magician, picks up his two buckets, and starts to tiptoe away. Mickey does not see the Sorcerer smile slightly. He takes his sixth tiptoe step on a harp note and is halfway out of the cavern on his seventh when the Sorcerer smacks him on the bottom with his own broom. Mickey hightails it out the doorway on the rapid one-two-three-Boom of the final four chords.

Deems Taylor watches Fred Moore, the "Mickey expert," draw the star of The Sorcerer's Apprentice. Marvin Woodward, who also animated Mickey, the Apprentice, received these instructions: "Work for a cute, short, chunky Mickey in this scene. Do not let him get too tall. He should not be over three heads high. When the first key poses have been drawn, please refer them to Fred Moore for possible suggestions. Fred Moore is assisting all animators in this picture in an attempt to make Mickey conform to a cute style."

**B**y 1937, Americans identified with Mickey Mouse, and the world identified Mickey with America. There were fifteen hundred Mickey Mouse clubs in the United States alone and others springing up worldwide. President Franklin D. Roosevelt wanted a Mickey Mouse cartoon included every time movies were shown at the White House, and the League of Nations called Mickey "an international symbol of good will." England's King George V refused to go to the movies unless a Mickey Mouse film was shown, and Queen Mary once came late to tea rather than miss the end of a charity showing of *Mickey's Nightmare.*

Along with Walt Disney, his creator and alter ego, Mickey embodied America's spirit of adventure, our insatiable curiosity, our love of innovation, and our optimistic belief that there was a happy solution to everything. Like Roosevelt's America, the only thing Mickey had to fear was fear itself.

Mickey Mouse was recapitulating our history in his cartoons, particularly our love of new technologies. It was fitting that when Walt tried the first sound-on-film cartoon with *Steamboat Willie* in 1928, Mickey made his first try at piloting a steamboat—and ended the voyage as a star. He burlesqued Lindbergh in *Plane Crazy* (1928); trainmen in *Mickey's Choo-Choo* (1929); teamsters in *The Plow Boy* (1929); and cowboys in *The Cactus Kid* (1930). He and Minnie Mouse crossed the continent in a covered wagon in *Pioneer Days* (1930). He engaged in athletic competition in *Barnyard Olympics* (1932); was an explorer (modeled after the real-life Trader Horn) in *Trader Mickey* (1932); a tourist in *Mickey in Arabia* (1932); a football player in *Touchdown Mickey* (1932); and a steamshovel operator in *Building a Building* (1933). He was *The Klondike Kid* (1932); *The Mail Pilot* (1933); and a hero in *Two-Gun Mickey* (1934), in which he rescued Minnie from bandits.

Like Walt, and most Americans in those days, he had a terrific curiosity, and he'd try almost anything. Confronted by a beanstalk, he climbed it (*Giantland,* 1933); a mirror, he went through it (*Thru the Mirror,* 1936); poltergeists, and he cleaned house (*Lonesome Ghosts,* 1937). He even conducted a band in the midst of a cyclone (*The Band Concert,* 1935), and brought the musicians back to earth safely—and on the beat.

Disney's composers set all this action to music, but action was king in the Mickey Mouse cartoons. On the other hand, in the Silly Symphonies, Disney's other cartoon series, the music was paramount. Here the action was drawn to fit original scores written by such Disney composers as Frank Churchill, Leigh Harline, and Albert Hay Malotte (who made a name for himself as the composer of a musical setting for "The Lord's Prayer").

Early in 1937, Disney decided to make a Silly Symphony set to a composition that already told a story and was recognized as music of quality. The musical story he picked was *The Sorcerer's Apprentice,* an ancient legend of a magician's assistant who experiments with his master's powers and discovers that he cannot control them. It was first written down by the Greek satirist Lucian in the second century. Early in the nineteenth century, Goethe wrote a ballad on the theme, which he titled *Der Zauberlehrling (The Apprentice Ma-*

*gician)*. In 1897, the French composer Paul Dukas used Goethe's poem as the basis for an orchestral scherzo, *L'Apprenti-sorcier*. In May, 1937, Walt Disney's agents contacted the American agent for Dukas's publisher about purchasing the rights to use the music in an animated cartoon.

By the end of July, Walt had the rights, and he was considering signing a well-known conductor to add still more prestige to the ambitious project.

One must wonder about the element of luck that now enters into Disney's adventure. As has been seen, Stokowski described his first meeting with Disney in a Los Angeles restaurant as a chance encounter. Thirty-four years later, in an interview with the editor of the *Royal College of Music Magazine* in London, Stokowski recalled how Disney "told me of a French composition about a kind of a great magician and a bad boy. He liked that music very much and so we discussed it. . . . He said, 'You know—how would you like the idea of making a picture of that? I have some thoughts of how that magician looked and how the bad boy looked and it is very picturesque, brilliant music.' So gradually we decided to do it and it was completed."

"I am all steamed up over the idea of Stokowski working with us on *The Sorcerer's Apprentice*," Disney wrote his representative on October 26, 1937—less than two months before the premiere of *Snow White.* "I feel that the possibilities of such a combination are so great that we could stretch a point and use his hundred men, as well as work out an arrangement to compensate him, personally, for his time—and we could well afford to record the music in any manner Stokowski would want to do it. . . . In fact, I think so much of the idea that I have already gone ahead and now have the story in work with this crew, on the chance that we will be able to get together with Stokowski and possibly have the music recorded within a short time. . . ."

Walt cast Mickey Mouse as the Sorcerer's Apprentice—and, suddenly, the motive force behind the Mickey Mouse and Silly Symphony cartoons merged into the apotheosis of the Disney cartoon: the best possible action with the best possible music.

When Walt got all steamed up, Walt's Studio got all steamed up. Walt assigned Perce Pearce as animation director for the project, with Carl Fallberg helping him on story, and Leigh Harline as musical director. (The following January, Walt had to take Pearce and Fallberg off *The Sorcerer's Apprentice* and assign them to set up a *Bambi* unit; he then chose James Algar, who had animated animals on *Snow White,* to direct the short.) To supervise the animation, Walt assigned the same team that had supervised the animation of the seven dwarfs, Mickey expert Fred Moore, and Vladimir "Bill" Tytla, who animated the Sorcerer himself. In order to give Mickey a greater range of expression, Moore gave him pupils in his eyes for the first time.

November 2, 1937, brought a letter from Stokowski: "I am thrilled at the idea of recording *The Sorcerer's Apprentice* with you, because you have no more enthusiastic admirer in the world than I am." By November 8, the first section of the rough continuity was ready; by November 9, section two.

On November 15, Perce Pearce provided all seven hundred

*An animation drawing of Mickey walking follows instructions. "Let him step high, wide, and handsome like an Elk on parade," storyman Perce Pearce told Les Clark.*

Perce Pearce explains Mickey's attitude as he leads the broom, then turns to see that it is following. "Mickey is cute and cocky. He has a big grin on his face . . . that's his attitude. On all this stuff . . . he is very serious. . . . It's not until he looks back and sees it working that he begins to grin. After he looks back, he's reassured and takes on the happy outlook and grins the rest of the scene."

members of the Disney staff with a synopsis of Goethe's ballad *Der Zauberlehrling (The Apprentice Magician)*: "The composer of the Sorcerer score based his music on a ballad by Goethe in which is described the predicament of an apprentice who appropriates the magic of his master, commands a broom to carry water for him, then discovers that he does not know how to stop the broom. When everything else fails, he chops the broom into splinters with an axe; each piece, however, magically rises to become a separate broom, continuing to carry water into the Sorcerer's castle, which is now becoming flooded. Only the intervention of the Sorcerer during a stirring 'command phrase' toward the end of the music brings things into order again." Goethe in a nutshell.

Walt Disney was always telling himself and others his stories over and over again, to see how briefly, clearly, and simply the theme could be stated. He once ran into animator Ward Kimball in the parking lot and told him the entire plot of *Dumbo* in three minutes. Now he told *The Sorcerer's Apprentice*, as he saw it, in three sentences:

"The thought is this: Mickey is an apprentice wanting the power of the Sorcerer to do his work. Then when that happens and he has that power, then he dreams of his great power. But when he awakens and finds what the broom has done and he hasn't the power to stop the broom, we find Mickey having to resort to an axe to try to stop the broom's work."

Walt Disney, now only five weeks away from the premiere of *Snow White,* was on the verge of having more money and power than he had ever had before. So it is perhaps not surprising that he was most interested in Mickey's dreams of power. Stenographer Bee Selck made a note after the November 13 story meeting that "Walt expressed himself about this dream several times by saying that Mickey could be here, there—anywhere. It is like a dream actually is. There doesn't need to be any flowing continuity."

Walt thought of "Mickey up there on that rock directing those planets and those comets and pulling up the ocean" as a caricature of a conductor. And he gave his ideas on the layout of those scenes: "Have a lot of up-shots, looking up at the guy, you know, like you'd shoot up at an orchestra conductor as he is conducting. Naturally, Stokowski doesn't burlesque, but we're caricature."

It was as if Walt were using Mickey to caricature himself and his dreams—the conductor of artists rather than musicians who now looks over a cliff into the future and sees that everything is possible.

The two paragraphs from the written continuity of November 6, 1937, dealing with Mickey's dream give as good a picture as we may ever get of a dreamer who suspects that his dreams are about to come spectacularly true:

"We leave the broom working, Mickey asleep, and dissolve into a dream sequence. In this we show Mickey going to fantastic lengths with his new power. It is the picture of the typical little man and what he would like to do once given complete control of the earth and its elements. In his dream Mickey is having a spectacular lot of

*A color sketch of Mickey's mood at the moment when the Sorcerer begins to leave him alone in the cavern—and the Apprentice already knows that he will try to bring the broom to life. In preparing* The Sorcerer's Apprentice, *careful attention was given to the psychological effects of color. Disney art director John Hubley liked to remind people that color reaches audiences with the speed of light, so it has its effect even faster than sound.*

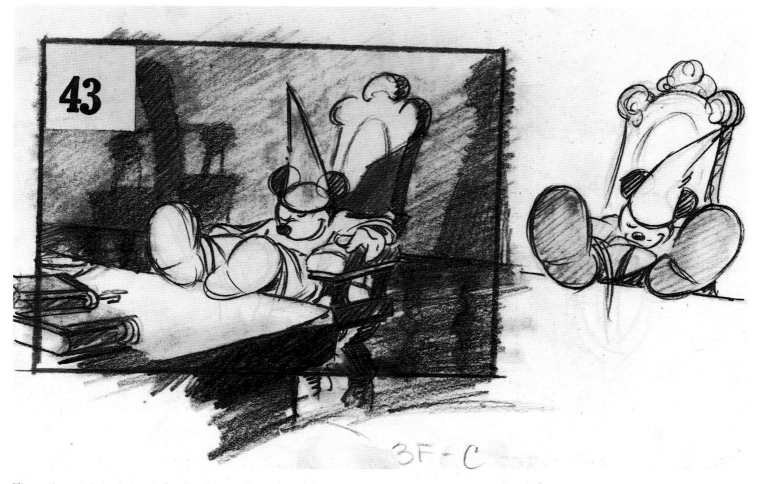

The early storyboard sketch for The Sorcerer's
Apprentice *(above)* shows a Disney artist imagining
how Mickey would go into his dream of power.
In the two frames *(opposite)*, we see the way Mickey
actually went to sleep and started to dream in
the finished film.

In a frame from the film, Mickey Mouse conducts the heavens (opposite). In the colored drawings (right), the story sketch artists visualize Mickey's dream broken down into long shots, close-ups, etc., and camera angles. The original sketches are each from four to five inches high. Their purpose was to give Walt what he wanted: a "picture of the typical little man and what he would like to do once given complete control of the earth and its elements. In his dream Mickey is having a spectacular lot of fun without being malicious."

Sc. 33 - M.C.U. Mickey beckoning
o.s. camera left.
(Sc. 33.11 - L.S. Planets roll in
from left to right, going out of
field overhead.)

Sc. 33.1 - M.C.U. Mickey beckoning
to o.s. camera right.
(Sc. 33.2 - L.S. Planets rolling in
from right to left overhead.)

Sc. 39.1 - C.U. Mickey gives dainty
dance commands then reaches to camera
left with big arm sweep to draw in
wave.

Sc. 40 - M.S. Pen with waves breaking
against cliff.

Sc. 10 - M.S. Still shot of broom in
corner - leaning against wall.

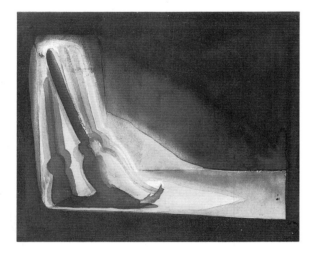

Sc. 11 - M.C.U. Mickey rolls up
sleeves - goes into first two
commands - on second command, pan
to broom in corner - faint glow
appears around it.

Sc. 20 - M.S. Mickey and broom leave
fountain.

Sc. 14 - C.U. Mickey in flutter
motion with hands. Pan to broom
quivering, coming to life - pan with
broom to Mickey and truck out.
Mickey brings broom between buckets,
commands arms on it.

*These story sketches evolved from the Story
Department's outline of November 16, 1937: "At this
point in the score we hear for the first time the
prominent 'command phrase' as Mickey turns his
power on the broom. The next few bars of music vividly
picture the broom coming to life. It advances from
the corner to a spot between Mickey's two buckets. It
is as though magic rays were leaving the ends of
Mickey's fingers and working on the broom. At another
command gesture from Mickey, two arms spring
out of the broom handle and pick up the buckets; the
straw takes on the aspects of two vague feet and
the familiar broom theme in the music begins. Mickey
leads the broom around the room, doing a little
dance step alongside. He leads the broom to the vat
and pantomimes that it must be filled. The broom
empties the full buckets into the vat."*

*Mickey brings the broom to life—and perhaps feels
something of what animator Les Clark felt
when he brought both Mickey and the broom to life.*

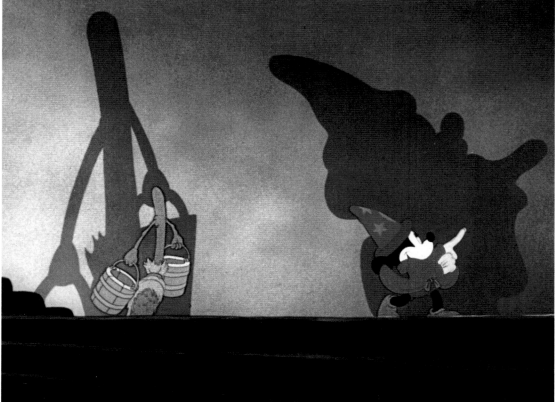

An oversize story sketch shows Mickey in two
positions as he conducts the broom to the vat. The
actual sketch is 13 inches long.

fun without being malicious. We see him strutting along a low skyline in silhouette, his shadow cast up into the clouds. . . .

"He struts to the brink of a cliff overlooking a calm sea; he whips it up to a rhythmic frenzy, waves dashing on the rocks as the music builds toward its climax. With a wave of his hand, Mickey causes huge storm clouds to gather over the ocean. His actions are those of a conductor leading a symphony orchestra of the elements. He points a finger to the left—a bolt of lightning flashes. He points in the other direction—another bolt of lightning explodes. He repeats the action with both hands at once and a terrific crash is heard overhead—each outburst to be synchronized with a dramatic spot in the music. Mickey is enjoying himself immensely. When he has whipped up a terrific storm, he calms everything down.

"At this point, we dissolve back to Mickey in the Sorcerer's chair. Still asleep, a huge smile of satisfaction spreads on his face. However, the room already is so full of water that Mickey's chair is beginning to float. . . ."

To give his artists a clear picture of what he wanted, Walt pulled two images out of his legendary visual memory. He urged them to make Mickey look "like Reginald Gardiner in *Broadway Melody of 1937,* I think it is—the one before his last one—the scene where he's a cop in the park and makes believe he's conducting an orchestra."

And Walt wanted Mickey to have some of the fire of an actual bandmaster he'd seen.

"Any you guys remember Creatore and his band?" he asked, recalling the bandmaster who would be immortalized twenty years later in the hit Broadway musical *The Music Man,* with its reference to "The Great Creatore" in the show-stopping *Seventy-Six Trombones* number.

"He had hair that stood right up," said Disney. "He was a big man—fiery. When he came on to conduct he always came in from the back and had to climb over chairs and players, kicking them aside. Coattails flying. Then a stiff bow. Then he'd really go at the music like a windmill." Walt's visual memory and eye for the movements that reveal personality were among the most important inspirations to the artists in his Studio because, as he said, "our most important aim is to develop definite personalities in our cartoon characters. Until a character becomes a personality, it cannot be believed—and belief is what I'm after."

In pursuit of believability, Disney constantly demonstrated to his artists the series of revealing gestures, such as those of the Great Creatore, that expressed the character's personality. And his artists constantly referred back to Walt's interpretation as they struggled to bring those characters to life on the screen.

Ironically, while Disney was investing Mickey's personality with his own dreams of power, Leopold Stokowski, on the East Coast, had been thinking about the personality of the Sorcerer's Apprentice, too, and the unexpectèd result of the maestro's thinking arrived in the mail on November 29:

"May I make a suggestion, which perhaps is entirely impractical or does not fit into your other ideas? What would you think of creating an entirely new personality for this film instead of

Sc. 50 - M.S. Command at foot of
stairs - broom over Mickey - pan
with broom thru knee deep water -
Mickey dives in - grabs bucket.

*In three storyboard sketches, Mickey tries to stop the broom. Note that the broom at this stage had an eye. In the finished film, it looks more threatening because it seems to see where it is going all too well without one.*

Sc. 59.1 - .U. Mickey's head -
brooms trampling on him.

Sc. 60 - M.S. Brooms stepping off
bottom step and surging toward vat.

Sc. 61 - M.C.U. Brooms pouring into
vat - vat overflowing a flood of
water.

Sc. 62 - M.L.S. Mickey down steps -
spies bucket, leaps into water -
picks up bucket, pan to window -
starts bailing.

Sc. 63 - M.L.S. Broom army pouring.

Sc. 64 - M.S. Mickey bailing again -
this time he is waist-deep.

Storyboard sketches detail Mickey's problems with
water. Depicting water convincingly was the problem of
the effects animator. In the scene (far left), a
medium shot of a whirlpool and spinning bucket,
Mickey pops up, spins around, gives a loud call (a horn
on the sound track), and splashes back into the
water. The water that floods the scene was the
creation of a dedicated Italian artist, Ugo D'Orsi.
D'Orsi was imagining—intuitively and persistently,
long before research photography could aid him—
patterns of waves and foam that looked, when
animated, powerful and wet.

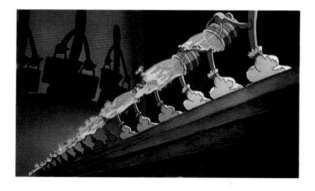

Mickey? A personality that could represent *you and me*—in other words, someone that would represent in the mind and heart of everyone seeing the film their own personality, so that they would enter into all the drama and emotional changes of the film in a most intense manner. You may have strong reasons for wishing Mickey to be the hero. But it seems to me that looking ahead into the future, there may be many films that you might wish to make with interesting, highly colored, emotional music background, and it might be well to create one or more new characters so as to enlarge the range of characterization. It seems to me that one of the most potent factors in the worldwide popularity of films is that the onlooker enters personally into the story and puts himself or herself in the place of the hero or heroine, and by doing so feels every moment of the drama. That is why I feel that if you create a new personality which represents every one of us, it might be a valuable factor in the years to come, and enlarge the scope. This is merely a suggestion, which . . . discard immediately if it does not interest you."

It definitely did not interest Disney. Before *Fantasia* was done, his Studio would create many new characters, enlarging its range of invention to include an undersized, out-of-step mushroom and the towering, prideful devil on top of Bald Mountain; but he ignored Stokowski's suggestion in his reply and in his production. Disney had the strongest possible reason for wanting Mickey to be the hero. He may have dressed him like Dopey, in a long robe and soft slippers, but the Mickey in *The Sorcerer's Apprentice* is Walt Disney at the time of *Fantasia,* having risen in just a few years from conducting a few associates in *The Band Concert* to becoming the dreamer on a mountaintop, conducting the stars. So, just as America identified with Mickey Mouse, and the world identified Mickey with America, so Walt Disney's identity was entwined with Mickey's. He dreamed Mickey's dream of being given "complete control of the earth and its elements"—a dream that resulted in Disneyland, Walt Disney World, and Epcot Center. And he built those parks and made his pictures on the dream that he and Mickey Mouse shared with his beloved Tom Sawyer and Huckleberry Finn: the dream of "having a spectacular lot of fun without being malicious."

The mythic irony of the experiment called *The Sorcerer's Apprentice* is that it didn't stop until it had turned into *Fantasia,* and by the time that dream was over, *Walt's* chair was beginning to float. *Fantasia* was a peaceful experiment in fusing pictures and music whose immediate success was doomed by World War II. Like a conflict in some Promethean myth, that war ended with the beginning of the nuclear age—the age in which man, like the Sorcerer's Apprentice, set in motion forces that can be as helpful or destructive as the animated brooms, and, like the brooms, may escape our control. It was said of the Disney version of *Three Little Pigs*—which set the nation to singing "Who's Afraid of the Big Bad Wolf?"—that it was the true folklore of the Great Depression of the 1930s. It now seems that *The Sorcerer's Apprentice,* which most people know in the Disney version, is the truest folklore of the nuclear age.

In the column of pictures (opposite), the broom divides and goes out of control in a graphic nightmare progression from realistic design to abstract to realistic again. The story sketch of Mickey spinning out of control in a whirlpool, and searching frantically in a book of magic for a way to save himself, is translated successfully into a frame from the finished film. Perhaps because of the tension of the scene, it contains the least-appreciated sight gag in Fantasia: the panic-stricken Apprentice, trying to find the formula to make all the water vanish, licks his finger to turn the page.

Carl Fallberg, who worked on story development with
Perce Pearce, recalled touring Hollywood costume
rental houses to find a robe and a pointed hat such as
a sorcerer might wear, and pasting white stars and
crescent moons on the hat. The Sorcerer wears
this costume in story sketches and an actual frame.
A frightened Mickey, his eyes almost as expressive as
the Sorcerer's, casts a glance toward his master (below).

Bill Tytla animated the Sorcerer in his many moods, from his magic conjurings to his allaying of the wild waters to his anger and spanking of Mickey. Slyly, Tytla gave the Sorcerer Walt's raised eyebrow of disapproval when he takes his magic hat back at the end—the expression that Walt himself called "that dirty Disney look" and that is seen in the anonymous caricature of Walt on page 200.

*Mickey Mouse congratulates Leopold Stokowski for conducting* The Sorcerer's Apprentice *— starring Mickey Mouse.*

*"The dinosaurs of Disney's* Fantasia *panting to their deaths across a desiccating landscape to the tune of Stravinsky's* Rite of Spring . . .*"*
—Stephen J. Gould

# SPRING

Igor Stravinsky composed *Le Sacre du printemps (Rite of Spring)* in 1912 as a pantomime-ballet. It was first performed a year later by Serge Diaghilev's Ballet Russe in Paris, with choreography that attempted to suggest tribal dances and rituals in prehistoric Russia. Stravinsky himself, however, never considered this the only possible interpretation of the work. "The pretext of the prehistoric birth of spring suggested to me the construction of the work," he wrote, but added: "The *Rite* exists as a piece of music first and last."

Walt Disney visualized *Rite of Spring* as a story of the evolution of life on Earth during the first billions of years of this planet's existence. His scenario is divided into eight sections:

*Trip Through Space.* We are to imagine ourselves out in space, looking down, from light-years away, on the planet Earth before there was any life on it. The camera takes us into a spiral nebula, past the sun, past a black nebula, comets, a red nebula, and a meteor, moving always toward the Earth, until it arrives amid spouting and exploding craters.

*Volcanoes.* Craters erupt. Hot lava flows. Rivers of lava reach the sea. The Earth cools.

*Undersea Life and Growth.* One-celled creatures appear, then hydras, annelid worms, jellyfish, trilobites; the first fish appear, then lungfish, capable of remaining alive with their heads out of water, then true amphibians. The fins of Polypterus change to legs, and he walks up a submerged rock to the surface of the ocean.

*Pterodactyls.* The flying reptiles of the Jurassic Period (which ended 136 million years ago) dive and glide again—a Mosasaur rises from a lagoon and pulls a Pterodactyl down underwater.

*Family Life.* The Age of the Dinosaurs. Feeding and child-rearing habits of Dimetrodon, Stegosaurus, Brontosaurus, Triceratops, and others.

*Fight.* Survival of the fittest. Stegosaurus was more than twice as big as an elephant and wore a heavy coat of scales, almost like a suit of armor. There were four huge spikes at the tip of his powerful tail. He is attacked by Tyrannosaurus Rex— King of the Tyrant Lizards—a dinosaur standing eighteen feet high and measuring about forty-seven feet overall. With his enormous jaws, lined with saber-sharp teeth six inches long, he brings Stegosaurus down and breaks his neck. Volcanoes rumble, warning of changes that will take place on Earth.

*Trek.* Dinosaurs pant their way to extinction through the terrible heat that is drying up water and green plants. This is a visualization of the late Cretaceous extinction some 70 million years ago, which set the stage for the era of mammals and the eventual evolution of man.

*Earthquake.* Earthquakes open huge crevices. Subterranean volcanoes burst to the surface of the oceans, creating giant tidal waves that engulf so many surviving creatures on land that the sea is once again the custodian of most of the life on Earth.

Trip Through Space. *Spiral nebula (top).*
*Eclipse of the sun (center). Earth and its moon seen*
*from outer space (bottom). No human being*
*had seen this sight in 1940, but Walt Disney was*
*determined to put it accurately on the screen.*

alt Disney's immediate and spontaneous reaction, the first time he heard Igor Stravinsky's *Le Sacre du printemps (Rite of Spring)*, is recorded in the minutes of the story meeting that took place on September 13, 1938.

"This is marvelous!" said Disney. "It would be perfect for prehistoric animals."

Up to that moment Disney and his associates had been considering Stravinsky's *Firebird* for inclusion in the Concert Feature, but Walt had then asked, "Was there ever anything written on which we might build something of a prehistoric theme—with prehistoric animals?"

"*Le Sacre du printemps* would be something on that order," Deems Taylor suggested, and a recording of Stravinsky's 1913 ballet music was played.

"There would be something terrific in dinosaurs, flying lizards, and prehistoric monsters," said Walt. "There could be beauty in the settings."

"A 'dawn of creation' theme," added Joe Grant, head of Disney's Character Model Department and, with Dick Huemer, story director of *Fantasia.*

As Walt showed more and more enthusiasm about a prehistoric sequence set to the *Rite of Spring* ballet music, whose original choreography concerned the ritual sacrifice of a maiden, Stokowski said, "Perhaps we could in some way retain the idea of a sacrifice. The jungle is full of sacrifice, animals preying upon each other, and being preyed upon—that is life. If we could put that on the screen and end with the most terrific and terrifying of the animals fighting and eating each other, people would gasp."

Disney responded enthusiastically to this suggestion. "We could base it on the 'dog eat dog' idea all the way through. We could have a battle and build it to a grand climax. It is the fight for life."

So Walt Disney chose *Rite of Spring* for *Fantasia*, based on a suggestion by Deems Taylor, not Stokowski. Stravinsky's widow, Vera, and Robert Craft, Stravinsky's friend and associate, were mistaken when they wrote in *Stravinsky in Pictures and Documents* that "The *Sacre* was undoubtedly Stokowski's, not Disney's choice," an assumption probably based upon the fact that "as early as 1927," Stokowski had written to Stravinsky telling him that he wished to study the score and, if Stravinsky was willing, to record it.

In actual fact, the choice of all the music in *Fantasia* was Disney's. At the Walt Disney Studio, the final decision on all matters rested with Walt Disney.

"He was absolute monarch there," said Huemer. "Why not? He made it."

It is certainly true, however, that Leopold Stokowski was an early champion of Stravinsky's most controversial score. Indeed, it was Stokowski who in 1930 gave *Rite of Spring* its first American performance, with Martha Graham dancing the role of the sacrificial victim in Léonide Massine's choreography. The famous premiere of *Sacre* in Paris in 1913 was perhaps the greatest scandal in the history of twentieth-century music, for, as Jean Cocteau described the scene:

"... people talked, booed, whistled, imitated animal cries. Perhaps they would have grown tired eventually if a group of aesthetes and some musicians had not been carried away by an excess of zeal and insulted, even jostled, the audience in the loges. The uproar degenerated into a pitched battle.

"Standing in her box, her diadem askew, the elderly Comtesse de Pourtalès brandished her fan and, in a positive frenzy, cried, 'This is the first time in sixty years that anyone has dared make fun of me!' The good lady was sincere; she really believed it was all a practical joke.

"And so we were introduced to this historic work in the midst of such tumult that the dancers could no longer hear the orchestra and had to take the beat from Nijinsky, who was prancing and yelling in the wings."

In 1938, twenty-five years after this tumultuous premiere, Stokowski acquainted Disney with the ballet's history: "This music has never been done justice to," he said. "It is too powerful. There was a terrific storm of protest when it was new. Critics sneer at it now, but you can't push it aside. We could cut it to about eighteen or nineteen minutes."

But, in fact, Disney used it at thirty minutes, though the sequence of the movements was altered to fit the continuity of the visual accompaniment.

Since Walt Disney, the movie producer with no formal training in music, responded enthusiastically to *Rite of Spring* the first time he heard it, it is amusing to read what Deems Taylor, the composer and critic, wrote about the work in 1920: "I'm not competent to discuss *Le Sacre du printemps,* as I have heard it only on the piano. But assuming . . . that Stravinsky is mechanism become music . . . I don't want it . . . I'm bored with imitations of noises . . . and their monotonous cacophony. Of course, it sounds like cacophony because I'm not used to it. . . ."

By 1938, Taylor had gotten used to it enough to suggest it to Disney as a piece "on which we might build something on a prehistoric theme." And this is the way that Taylor justified the music's new scenario when he introduced the piece in *Fantasia:* "When Igor Stravinsky wrote his ballet, *The Rite of Spring,* his purpose was — in his own words — 'to express primitive life.' And so, Walt Disney and his fellow artists have taken him at his word. Instead of presenting the ballet in its original form, as a simple series of tribal dances, they have visualized it as a pageant — as the story of the growth of life on earth: a coldly accurate reproduction of what scientists now think went on . . . the first few billion years of this planet's existence."

Earlier in that same September 13, 1938, story meeting, when Disney listened to Shostakovich's *Age of Steel,* and considered making "a montage effect of a building being erected or something" to that music, Walt had asked Stokowski: "Should we stick as closely as possible to the original ideas behind this music?" And Stokowski had replied, "Composers are not a bit strict about those things. They write for a certain idea, but when you suggest something else, they

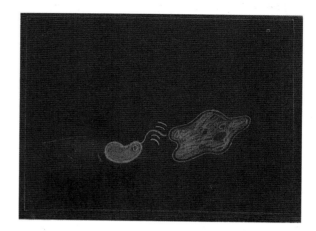

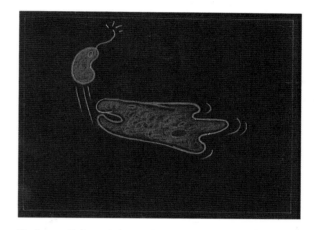

Undersea Life and Growth. *"Flagellate bumps into amoeba" (top) and "Flagellate scrams as amoeba tries to catch him" (bottom)—a Studio description of the scene animated by John McManus.*

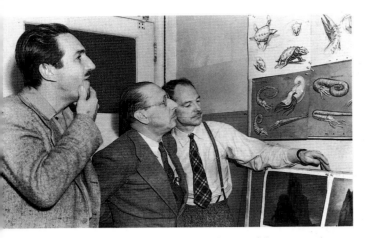

*Igor Stravinsky, composer of* Rite of Spring, *and Walt Disney are shown inspirational sketches for its story by Bill Roberts, co-director of the segment. The appearance of Roberts, visibly perspiring on a day when it was cool enough for Disney and Stravinsky to wear jackets, suggests that the job of a Disney director was not without its tensions and anxieties.*

are likely to agree. We shouldn't worry, if the spirit of the music is with us."

The subsequent history of the relationship between Walt Disney and Igor Stravinsky is a fascinating account of a composer who first wasn't—and then was—"strict about those things."

By the end of the meeting at which *Rite of Spring* was first played, Disney, Stokowski, and Taylor were all in agreement that making a visual accompaniment to Stravinsky's music was an important thing to do.

"I think you can bring this music to the consciousness of people so they will see how great it really is," said Stokowski. "At present, they are trying to down it. The men who are not creators sneer at it."

And Taylor added: "The great handicap that it has labored under is that it is not absolute music. It was written for motion and sight and when it is played in the concert hall, you only half hear it. The motion is right in the music."

Joe Grant had warned that "no matter how well we do prehistoric animals in our medium, people will laugh at them—they are just built for laughs. It is a theme that requires humor." Grant was no doubt recalling that one of the earliest animated films, Winsor McCay's 1909 *Gertie the Dinosaur*, had portrayed prehistoric creatures strictly for laughs; and in all the years since, dinosaurs had appeared in cartoons only as comical characters. Considering Disney's personality, that was probably an additional reason for him to take the new road.

So Walt put the question to Stokowski: "Should we take this dramatic theme?"

"That would be the idea behind it," said Stokowski—and that was the idea behind it.

The Disney Studio was already in communication with Stravinsky. On April 12, 1938, when *Fantasia*'s music was still being selected, a Disney agent had asked Stravinsky's publisher for permission to use *The Firebird* in the Concert Feature. Nothing came of this inspiration, but when Disney requested the film rights to *Rite of Spring*, Stravinsky instructed his New York attorney to sign a contract with Walt Disney Productions for "the irrevocable right, license, privilege, and authority to record in any manner, medium or form *Rites* [sic] *of Spring* for use in the film *Fantasia*."

The contract was signed January 4, 1939. The sum paid, according to Craft and Mrs. Stravinsky, was six thousand dollars. Just before Christmas that year, Stravinsky visited the Disney Studio in the company of the choreographer George Balanchine. He was shown *The Sorcerer's Apprentice*, which he told Disney he liked; and storyboards and models for *Rite of Spring*, which was then being animated. He posed for many pictures with Disney and his artists, and even took time out to joke with one of the animators working to his music.

"We were having our Christmas party," remembered Wolfgang Reitherman. "I was animating the dinosaurs at the time, and after a few drinks, I went into my room and started running the

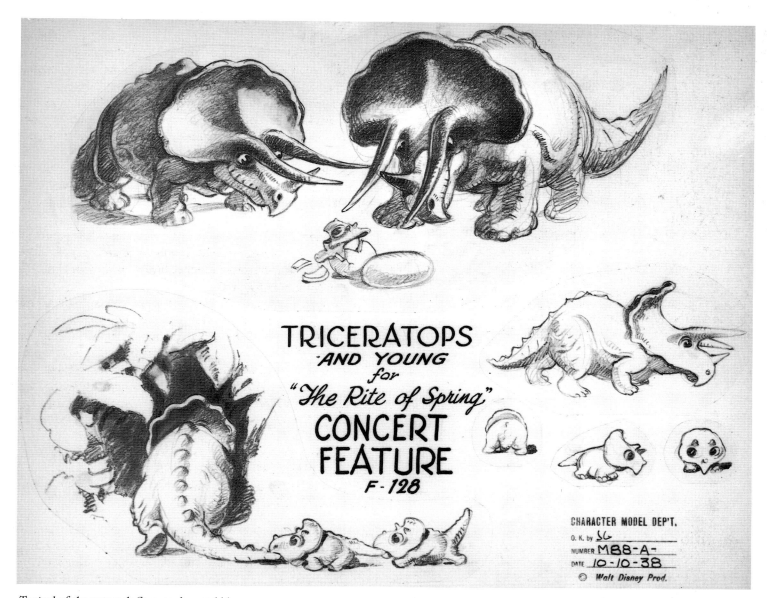

TRICERATOPS
AND YOUNG
for
"The Rite of Spring"
CONCERT
FEATURE
F-128

CHARACTER MODEL DEP'T.
O. K. by SG
NUMBER M88-A-
DATE 10-10-38
© Walt Disney Prod.

Typical of the artwork Stravinsky could have seen on this visit to the Studio just before Christmas, 1939, are the drawings, storyboards, and pastel sketches on these and the following two pages.

Deems Taylor, who introduced Fantasia's musical selections, and Leopold Stokowski, who conducted them, hold a model of a Triceratops head made to help animators visualize the creature. The storyboards behind them not only detail the action of Rite of Spring in sketches, but break down the prehistoric period into Ages. The color sketch (opposite) is of a newly hatched Triceratops, a dinosaur of the late Cretaceous Period of the Mesozoic Era that emerged from his shell some 70 million to 135 million years ago.

For months Disney artists listened to the recording of
Rite of Spring and drew prehistoric creatures. In a
memo written in 1935 to Don Graham, head of
the Disney training school, Walt had said: "I think a
good study of music would be indispensable to
the animator—a realization on their part of how
primitive music is, how natural it is for people to want
to go to music—a study of rhythm, the dance—the
various rhythms that enter into our lives every
day—how rhythmic the body really is—and how well
balanced. . . . That, in itself, is music. In other
words, it could be music in the body." For Rite of
Spring, director Bill Roberts, layout artist Dick Kelsey,
and animators Don Patterson and Art Palmer
fashioned a whole sequence around the consonance of
the swooping action of Pterodactyls and swooping
sounds in the Stravinsky score.

*Inspirational sketches for dinosaurs (above). Wolfgang "Woolie" Reitherman consults a three-dimensional model of Tyrannosaurus Rex as he animates Rite of Spring's climactic battle between a Stegosaurus and the King of the Tyrant Lizards (opposite, above).*

sound track to *Rite of Spring*—backward. You didn't hear any melody, but you sure heard some pretty dynamic sounds. I was enjoying it. Suddenly, the door opened, and there was Walt with Igor Stravinsky. Stravinsky was very nice about it. He said, 'Sounds good backward, too!' "

According to Craft and the composer's widow, Stravinsky was shown the finished film of *Rite of Spring* on October 12, 1940. They say that eleven days after this preview, on October 23, "two Disney directors called on the composer to discuss the possibility of making an animated film of *Renard*," Stravinsky's comic score about a fox in the barnyard. On October 28, Stravinsky sold an option to Disney not only for *Renard*, but also for *Fireworks* and *The Firebird*.

In later years, Stravinsky was quoted as being critical of the Disney version of *Rite of Spring*. The Champaign-Urbana (Ill.) *Courier*, in an interview with Stravinsky published March 3, 1949, reported that "Stravinsky spoke of Walt Disney's treatment of his music in *Fantasia* as terrible. 'I saw part of it at the Studio and walked out.' "

Craft and Vera Stravinsky explain the fact that the composer subsequently signed more contracts to have his music used in more Disney films by saying that he "sold the option . . . probably realizing that the music would never be used."

It is difficult to see how Stravinsky could have thought, when he sold Disney the option seventeen days before *Fantasia* was premiered, to use three more of his compositions in films, that the music would not be used. At that time Disney was so confident that *Fantasia* was going to be a financial success on its first release that work was already going forward on a second *Fantasia*, which was to include a Disney version of Prokofiev's *Peter and the Wolf*.

Disney's daughter, Diane Disney Miller, remembers being told that "when Prokofiev visited the United States he'd come to see Father with the unpublished score of *Peter and the Wolf*, and he said, 'I've composed this with the hope that someday you'll make a cartoon using my music.' " Disney and Stokowski had already begun planning *Peter and the Wolf* in story meetings for the second *Fantasia*, and when the project was abandoned because the original film failed to earn back its investment on its first release, Walt still completed *Peter and the Wolf* and released it as part of a 1946 film called *Make Mine Music*, composed mainly of pop music.

In that same year, Stravinsky expressed his philosophy toward what Stokowski called "music for all of us" in an article in *Musical Digest*: "When Walt Disney used *Le Sacre du printemps* for *Fantasia*, he told me: 'Think of the numbers of people who will now be able to hear your music.' Well, the numbers of people who consume music is of interest to somebody like Mr. Hurok [Sol Hurok, the concert impresario], but it is of no interest to me. The mass adds nothing to art. It cannot raise the level, and the artist who aims consciously at mass appeal can do so only by lowering his own level. The soul of each individual who listens to my music is important to me, not the mass feeling of a group. Music cannot be helped by means of an increase of the quantity of listeners, be this increase effected by the

In 1940, Igor Stravinsky autographed this photograph to Walt Disney "from an admirer of your great achievements" (below). The picture was taken when Stravinsky visited the Disney Studio just before Christmas, 1939, saw The Sorcerer's Apprentice, heard Stokowski's sound track for Rite of Spring, *then in production, and saw inspirational sketches for its visualization.*

film or any other other medium. It can be helped only through an increase in the quality of listening, the quality of the individual soul."

One man's individual soul was saddened when reading that. He thought of growing up in rural Illinois during World War II, and of being introduced to Stravinsky's music by *Fantasia*; then saving up to buy a record of Stravinsky himself conducting *Rite of Spring*; then going on to buy *Petrouchka* and *Firebird*; and of how, as a grown man, he finally *saw* Stravinsky conduct his own works, and was part of the standing ovation given the eighty-four-year-old composer after his farewell concert in Chicago. And this man thought of how another Disney cartoon, called *The Whale Who Wanted to Sing at the Met*, started him listening to the Metropolitan Opera radio broadcasts on Saturday afternoons. Stravinsky, whose father was the leading basso at the Imperial Opera House in St. Petersburg, who had two grand pianos in the family drawing room, perhaps had no need for *Fantasia*. He was in a position to insist that "music cannot be helped by means of an increase of the quantity of listeners"; but the quality of listening in Winnebago County, Illinois, depended upon having music of quality to listen to, even in the small towns of America.

*Animators' line drawings of dinosaurs feeding and browsing in a swamp magically recreated, when inked and painted and projected along with Stravinsky's music, give a feeling of the prehistoric world.*

For a generation after World War II, it was no longer fashionable among intellectuals to appreciate Disney. But the mood when Stravinsky signed his second contract with Disney was very different. We see it in the *Time* magazine cover story on *Fantasia* in November, 1940, written before it became apparent that the mass audience was not yet ready after all to accept *Fantasia*:

"An imposing list of top-flight contemporary composers (Paul Hindemith, Serge Prokofiev, William Grant Still, Deems Taylor, et al.) have vowed that they would spend their lives working for Disney if he would give them the chance. Composer Igor Stravinsky himself had signed a contract to do more music with Disney, has blandly averred that Disney's paleontological cataclysm was what he had in mind all along in his *Rite of Spring*."

From the outset, *Rite of Spring* was conceived as a scientific document," said John Hubley, who was the art director of three of the segment's eight sections (*Trip Through Space, Volcanoes,* and *Earthquake*). Walt explained what he wanted in fifteen simple words: "As though the studio had sent an expedition back to the earth 6,000,000 years ago."

To create the illusion of a trip through space in those days before the space age, Disney's Special Effects Department did some of its most imaginative work. First of all, animating a thousand stars in their courses would create an effect that would not be equal to the time it would take. Therefore, a model of the Earth was made from a thirty-watt Mazda light globe, about eighteen inches in diameter, painted red. It revolved and was illuminated in such a way as to show its craters to best advantage. This "Earth" was suspended at the end of a darkened room about twenty feet long. In this room the effects animators had created a little universe of stars. First they hung shining beads of various sizes at the ends of threads of various lengths. At the end of the room, behind the Earth, was a dark screen. This screen was punctured with innumerable small holes and illuminated from behind. When a 35-mm movie camera trucked through the bead-stars toward the light-globe Earth, the pinholes of light gave the illusion of an infinity of stars twinkling beyond our planet. This "million-mile" truck through space was the answer of Disney's artists to Walt's vision two years before when he thought about the opening of *Rite of Spring* and said, "Boy, you'll really go through space. . . . I think it would be a terrific idea—that idea of endless space."

Since so many of the visuals in *Rite of Spring* were aimed at reproducing the appearance of things never seen, or not seen in such a form, careful studies were made of existing archeological reconstructions and prehistoric lore. "So intense became this paleontological hunger," wrote Hubley, "that contact with museums and Ph.D.s was established. Here's a characteristic *Rite of Spring* request: 'Please provide anything and everything pertaining to the Permian Age through the Triassic which covers development from amphibians to earliest reptile forms. Note Grantops, Scymnognathus, Seymouria, Cynognathus and relating forms.' " The Studio later said that "such world-famous authorities as Roy Chapman Andrews, Ju-

When Julian Huxley, the world-famous biologist, came to the Studio to talk about dinosaurs, the Disney artists turned him into one. They evolved a "Huxleyranodon," a creature with a dinosaur's tail and Huxley's glasses, sharp nose, and unkempt hair.

HUXLEYRANODON

lian Huxley, Barnum Brown and Edwin P. Hubble volunteered helpful data and became enthusiastic followers of the picture's progress."

One of the problems, for example, was how to picture the primeval convulsions of the Earth's surface. Josh Meador, who supervised the animation of the special effects, found a way to show mud pots bubbling and breaking and splashing that resulted in convincing movement on the screen. First he mixed a gummy mess of oatmeal, mud, and coffee in a vat. Then he sent bubbles up through it with air hoses. High-speed cameras photographed this action. The individual frames were processed on cels dyed red against a yellow background. Animation was added to create more splashes and broaden the action. All this was photographed against backgrounds with controlled light intensities.

At the beginning, the animators had trouble visualizing the scale of the dinosaurs. Bill Roberts, codirector of *Rite of Spring* with Paul Satterfield, peered over his wire-rimmed eyeglasses and offered them this advice: "Just draw a twelve-story building in perspective, then convert it into a dinosaur and animate it."

How well the dinosaurs turned out can be proved by the fact that nationally known scientists, seeing *Fantasia,* have concurred that prehistoric life becomes an exciting reality through Disney's unique medium. "The New York Academy of Science asked for a private showing of *Rite of Spring*," reported *Time,* "because they thought its dinosaurs better science than whole museum loads of fossils and taxidermy."

Roberts decided that the most effective way of suggesting the immensity of a beast that measured forty-seven feet long and eighteen feet high would be to have the audience gaze up at it from below. So the camera level was kept low, which was particularly effective in the battle at the end. Stokowski, remember, had told Disney that "if we could . . . end with the most terrific and terrifying of the animals fighting and eating each other, people would gasp." Discussing such a battle at an early story meeting, one storyman suggested using the Triceratops.

"No," broke in another, who obviously knew his dinosaurs, "we want to use the Stegosaurus because of this action of his tail with the four spikes."

So it became a battle between Stegosaurus and "the most terrific and terrifying" of all dinosaurs, Tyrannosaurus Rex.

No human being, of course, had ever seen the "action" of a Stegosaurus's tail. While scientists have been able to reconstruct the skeletons of the dinosaurs so that we have an accurate picture of their size and shape and weight, it was not until the Disney artists combined their study of the skeletal remains with their animators' knowledge of balance and weight that anyone had an educated visualization of how these creatures might have moved.

"When we first started on the *Rite of Spring*," said art director Dick Kelsey, "it was the general consensus that it was to be very dark and moody, but it appeared that as it progressed and they began to evaluate the animation more highly, they gradually eliminated the mood and replaced it with clarity of action."

*Stokowski described the Disney version of the young Earth as "imagination based on facts" and, in fact, Disney and his artists listened to Stokowski's recording of the Stravinsky score and heard lava and volcanoes. As Walt explained it, "When we ran into that music yesterday, in the middle of the first half comes a sort of place where hell breaks loose, and that could be the age where the skies become dark and the earth internally erupts. . . . We could have volcanoes erupting, and terrific amounts of smoke."*

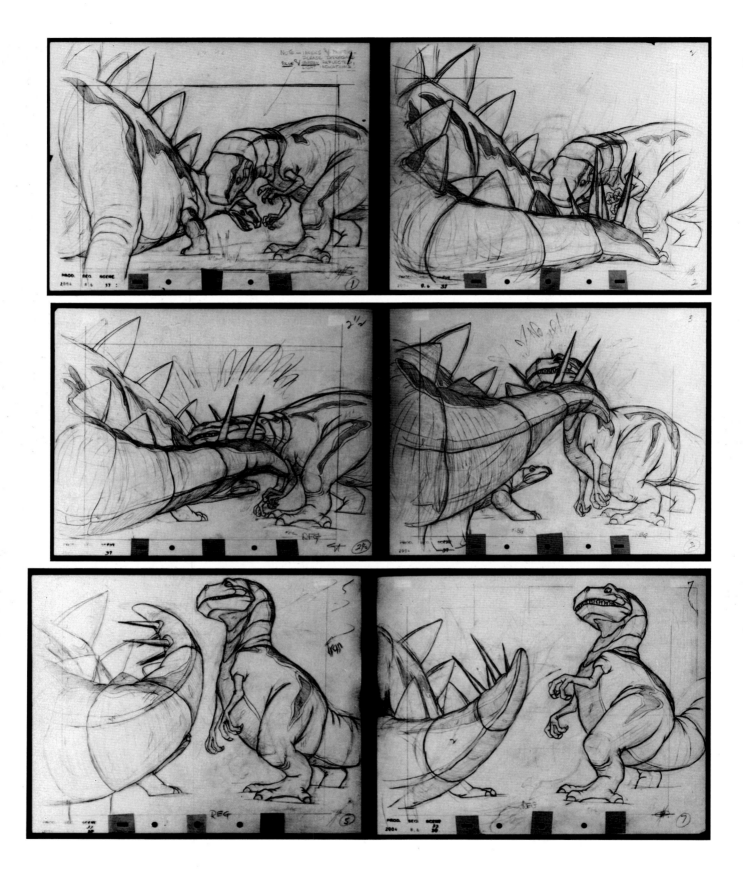

When Woolie Reitherman was animating the dinosaurs, Walt cautioned him against anthropomorphism — heretofore a strength of Disney animal animation. "Don't make them cute animal personalities. They've got small brains, y'know; make them real!" No human being had ever seen a real dinosaur, of course; but Woolie, working closely with director Bill Roberts, imagined the battle to the death between a Stegosaurus and Tyrannosaurus Rex, pictured on these pages, that has since satisfied the imaginations of millions of other human beings. (Note the convincing follow-through on the swipe of the Stegosaurus's powerful tail. Museums have reconstructed such tails, but no one has ever seen one in action.)

Assigning artists to make prehistoric creatures live
again through the magic of animated drawings
was typical of Walt Disney's approach to education.
And the day arrived when the New York Academy of
Science had a private showing of the Rite of Spring
segment, because it found that Disney's dinosaurs
served science better than museums full of fossils and
taxidermy. The research of the Studio's artists had
resulted in an unforgettable image: Tyrannosaurus Rex
defying the elements.

Goethe once said, "All that is alive tends toward color, individuality, specificity, effectiveness and opacity; all that is done with life inclines toward knowledge, abstraction, generality, transfiguration and transparency." The Disney artists gradually visualized specific dinosaurs who were individuals of a certain effective shape (Diplodocus had a long neck: he could eat his dinner from the treetops) and opaque color (Tyrannosaurus Rex, the tyrant king of the dinosaurs, is a black shape with blood-red eyes and mouth). When the animators took the next step and visualized these creatures in motion, they transformed prehistoric monsters from creatures who had long been done with life to creatures who were once again alive.

The scheme of this segment is a good example of the proper use of animation: to show things that are beyond the capabilities of live-action film. It imaginatively pictures the process of evolution from the time when this planet was still a molten mass to the point where the dinosaurs disappeared from the face of the earth.

Pare Lorentz, a major figure in the development of the documentary film (*The Plow That Broke the Plains* and *The River*), saw the importance of *Rite of Spring* as a document of that which could not otherwise be documented, calling it "the most extraordinary motion picture I've ever seen on the screen; it is by far the most daring, powerful, exciting and successful portion of *Fantasia*."

But it took a generation for it to become clear what the impact of *Fantasia*'s *Rite of Spring* had been.

Disney had originally intended to carry his screen story beyond the death of the dinosaurs, through "The Age of Mammals and the First Men" to "Fire and the Triumph of Man." But the fundamentalists, according to John Hubley, threatened to make trouble for *Fantasia* if Walt connected evolution with human beings. Disney thereupon decided that *Fantasia* might have enough trouble getting accepted by the general public—as indeed it did—without courting a creationist boycott. Ideas similar to those contained in the Disney Studio's 1938 outline of "Part 3—Fire and the Triumph of Man" finally reached the screen over forty years later in the 1981 film *Quest for Fire* without causing problems.

The death of the dinosaurs, however, was brought to the screen most memorably by *Fantasia*. "No problem in paleontology has attracted more attention or led to more frustration than the search for causes of these extinctions," wrote the Harvard paleontologist Stephen J. Gould. "Nor has the problem escaped public notice. I remember well my first exposure to it at age five: the dinosaurs of Disney's *Fantasia* panting to their deaths across a desiccating landscape to the tune of Stravinksy's *Rite of Spring*."

What better testimony to the educational value of *Fantasia*'s prehistoric segment could there be than the recollection of one of science's leading paleontologists that his earliest inspiration was *Rite of Spring*? What tribute to *Rite of Spring* could be more touching than the dedication of Professor Gould's book *Ever Since Darwin: Reflections in Natural History*:

"For my father, who took me to see the Tyrannosaurus when I was five."

*According to Harvard paleontologist Stephen J. Gould, "The late Cretaceous extinction, some 70 million years ago . . . cleared the earth of its dominant terrestrial animals, the dinosaurs and their kin—thus setting a stage for the dominance of mammals." Millions of human beings have become aware of this mass extinction through Disney's visualization of it in these images.*

# INTERMISSION:

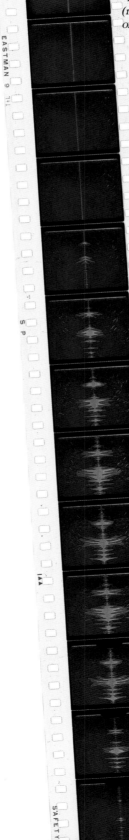

*Sound Track*

*"Bronx cheer"
(raspberry-colored,
of course)*

**F**antasia's intermission feature is as unusual as the program itself. The Disney artists, sensitive to all visual patterns, were fascinated by the *look* of the sound track, which is a narrow band on the left side of the film, where the emulsion faces the viewer. This band carries recorded patterns that are activated during projection to recreate dialogue, narration, music, and sound effects. Every sound has a pattern of its own, and Disney decided to create animation based on those patterns. Then, being Disney, he endowed the sound track with a personality. The Sound Track would be a shy but proud vibrating line who would move, for once, to center screen and show audiences how he makes his sounds. *Fantasia*'s narrator was used to coax this anthropomorphized Sound Track away from the sidelines, and these are the exchanges that transpired:

# THE SOUND TRACK

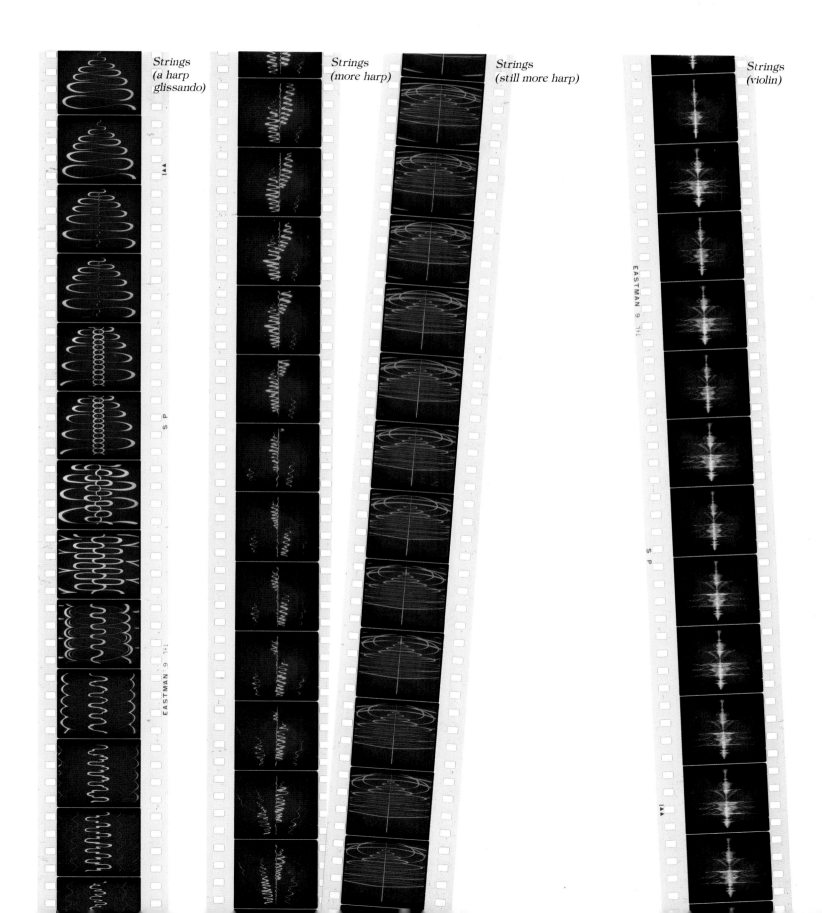

Strings
(a harp
glissando)

Strings
(more harp)

Strings
(still more harp)

Strings
(violin)

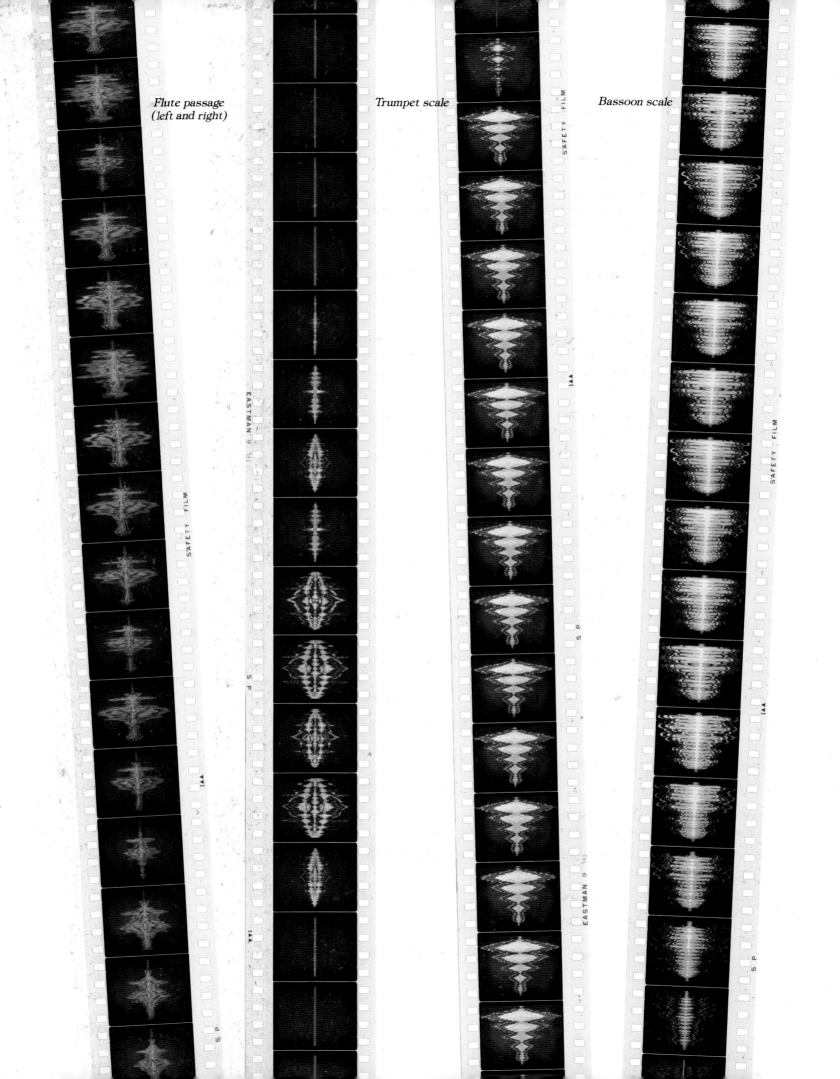

Flute passage
(left and right)

Trumpet scale

Bassoon scale

NARRATOR: Before we get into the second half of the program, I'd like to introduce somebody to you. Somebody who is very important to *Fantasia*. He's very shy, and very retiring. I just happened to run across him one day at the Disney Studios. But when I did, I realized that he was not only an indispensable member of the organization, but a screen personality whose possibilities nobody around the place had ever noticed. And so, I am very happy to have this opportunity to introduce to you—the Sound Track.

THE SOUND TRACK: *peeks shyly out, then ducks back.*

NARRATOR: All right . . . come on . . . it's all right. Come on. Don't be timid . . .

THE SOUND TRACK: *comes timidly to the center of the screen.*

NARRATOR: Atta Sound Track! Now, watching him, I discovered that every beautiful sound also creates an equally beautiful picture. Now look—will the Sound Track kindly produce a sound? Go on, don't be nervous. Go ahead—any sound—

THE SOUND TRACK: *produces a razzberry—a "Bronx cheer"—then snaps back to his normal vibrating position.*

NARRATOR: Well, that isn't quite what I had in mind. Suppose we see and hear the harp.

THE SOUND TRACK: *produces a harp glissando.*

NARRATOR: Good. Now one of the strings. Say—oh, the violin.

THE SOUND TRACK: *produces violin sounds.*

NARRATOR: And now one of the woodwinds—the flute . . .

THE SOUND TRACK: *produces a flute passage.*

NARRATOR: Very pretty. Ah—now let's have a brass instrument—the trumpet.

THE SOUND TRACK: *runs a trumpet scale, strains at the top note, but finally makes it.*

NARRATOR: All right. Now, how about a low instrument? The bassoon?

THE SOUND TRACK: *runs down the bassoon scale, spreads out, then pauses.*

NARRATOR: Go on. Drop the other shoe, will you?

THE SOUND TRACK: *finally hits a very, very low bassoon note.*

NARRATOR: Oh, thanks. Well, now to finish, suppose we see some of the percussion instruments. Beginning with the bass drum . . .

THE SOUND TRACK: *produces, in rapid succession, bass drum, cymbal, snare drum, and triangle.*

NARRATOR: Thanks ever so much, old man.

THE SOUND TRACK: *makes an uncertain, bashful exit.*

The theater darkens, and the orchestra gets ready to begin *The Pastoral Symphony.*

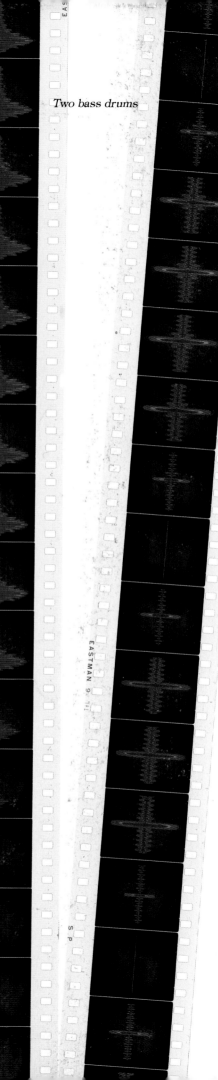

Two bass drums

# THE PASTORAL

*Diana, goddess of the moon, fades in and shoots a comet.*

# SYMPHONY

Ludwig van Beethoven's Sixth Symphony, *The Pastoral Symphony*, was composed between 1807 and 1808, and was first performed in Vienna in the latter year. Beethoven gave it the subtitle *Recollections of Country Life*, and also provided each movement with a title, several of them similar to the ones that Disney and his artists later chose for the action they imagined for the music.

1. *Awakening of Pleasant Feelings upon Arriving in the Country, Allegro ma non troppo*, is *Mount Olympus* in *Fantasia*. The countryside of Beethoven's fancy becomes the Elysian Fields at the foot of Mount Olympus, home of the Greek gods. The pleasant feelings are awakened in creatures of mythology—mischievous fauns, baby unicorns, and winged horses. Much of the movement is concerned with the playful flying and swimming of Pegasus, the black, winged stallion, his snow-white mate, and their four foals, including Baby Pegasus.

2. *Scene by the Brook, Andante molto mosso*, becomes *Centaurs and Centaurettes* —the latter a name Disney coined for the female centaurs—but the brook remains. Beethoven wrote musical suggestions of a peaceful brook rippling over stones and the growling of a thunderstorm, and Disney pictures both. By the brook, the centaurettes amuse themselves fashioning hats out of flowers, bark, and doves, and it is here that they are courted by a band of husky centaurs. The movement ends with winged cupids piping a sad and lonely centaur into the presence of Melinda, clearly the centaurette of his dreams.

3. *Peasants' Merrymaking, Allegro*, becomes *Bacchanal*. The merrymakers here are Bacchus, the god of wine, who rides tipsily out of the forest on his donkey-unicorn, Jacchus, and all the mythological creatures who join him in the Bacchanal, they pressing wine from grapes, he drinking it, and cavorting.

4. *The Storm, Allegro*, stays just that. In Disney's storm, the sky darkens, rain begins to fall, and a bearded Zeus appears in the clouds above the revelers. He takes lightning bolts forged by Vulcan and hurls them at Bacchus, finally shattering the wine vat and causing a flood of wine. Then, tiring of the sport, Zeus lies down in the clouds to sleep, folding it around him like a blanket.

5. *Shepherd's Hymn of Thanksgiving After the Storm, Allegretto*, becomes, simply, *Sunset*. After the storm Iris floats across the sky, trailing her rainbow behind her. Pan, Cupid, and Baby Pegasus play in the rainbow's colors. Apollo rides his chariot of the sun, driving three great horses, waving to the merrymakers, who wave back thankfully for the lovely day now ending. Morpheus brings on the night sky as he crosses the horizon. Diana grasps the new moon as if it were a bow and fires a comet that scatters stars. The stars fall into their places in the night sky, and the camera trucks back to show the Elysian Fields and Mount Olympus (the recurrent towering podium shape) at peace under the moon and the stars.

F. Scott Fitzgerald described guests who came to Gatsby's parties "with a simplicity of heart that was its own ticket of admission." That was the way Walt Disney approached Art's portals. "Perhaps Bach and Beethoven are strange bedfellows for Mickey Mouse," he wrote, "but it's all been a lot of fun, and I want to thank Leopold Stokowski, Deems Taylor, and all my coworkers for holding my head up when the water got too deep."

The cultural waters were deepest in the short film animated to Beethoven's *Pastoral Symphony.* It was the most widely criticized selection on the *Fantasia* program, the consensus being that the visual complement was not worthy of the spirit of the music. An even more fundamental criticism, however, was that such music as *The Pastoral Symphony* should not have any visual complement at all.

George Balanchine, the New York City Ballet's longtime choreographer/artistic director, once told why some music is not co-expressible with visible action: "In listening to composers like Beethoven and Brahms, every listener has his own ideas, paints his own picture of what the music represents. Beethoven did not have this in mind, I am sure, but he does seem to be painting a picture and people like to put themselves in that picture. Now how can I, a choreographer, try to squeeze a dancing body into a picture that already exists in somebody's mind? It simply won't work."

The ironic thing, however, is that the Disney artists did not originally plan *Fantasia*'s mythological segment with *The Pastoral Symphony* in mind. The music originally chosen to go with their animations of fauns and centaurs and flying horses was Pierné's *Cydalise.* Walt loved the story continuity that was developing in the story sketches he saw at meetings with his artists, and particularly he admired the sketches of the flying horses. But the Pierné music didn't seem to be working well with these images. And so, at the story meeting on November 2, 1938, we find Disney's decision to abandon the Pierné piece and search for some other music.

"I think that is marvelous," said Walt, looking at a sketch of Pegasus, "the way the horse comes down . . . with his feet out and lands in the water. When he lands, I would like to see those wings fold like a swan's."

Walt had now found the reference point in reality that is behind all good animated fantasy: when the flying horses swim in the water, they will fold their wings like swans. As he so often did, Disney provided his artists with a visual clue — which they quickly proceeded to develop.

Dick Huemer, one of *Fantasia*'s two story directors, who ultimately suggested using *The Pastoral Symphony,* was now following the line of Walt's thinking: if a flying horse folds its wings like a swan, mightn't it also put its head underwater like a swan?

"You mean the way the bird does with his beak?" asked Huemer, after consulting his visual memory. "They bite themselves, too, like they have fleas."

"Horses don't have fleas," said Walt flatly. "They bite at flies." Whenever he was discussing the animation of animals, his mind went back to the farm animals he had observed in Marceline,

Missouri, when he was between five and nine years old. And his recall, said his associates, was nearly total.

And now Walt's imagination was blossoming: "A very effective thing as they swim along is to keep the horse's tail swimming. One tail floating on the water like hair."

Suddenly, Walt thought that they had enough for this sequence: "I think that stuff is new enough, fresh enough to an audience that it would be good not to overcrowd it with business."

But Walt Disney had a far bigger problem with *Fantasia's* venture into mythology, though he didn't bring it up at that meeting until he had approved most of the action that had been designed for the sequence.

"The thing I keep thinking about, too—the material is so damn good in here—I wonder if we couldn't make our own conglomeration."

Realizing that Walt was dissatisfied with the music, Joe Grant admitted that it was hampering the development of the story. "Every time we get going with some ideas, we have to stop."

That was the cue for Walt to say flatly what he was thinking: "This music is not so hot to me. . . . We should find music to fit the things we have in mind here—but good music."

At that point Huemer suggested that Disney "hire Stravinsky or this man Pierné" to write some original music for the mythological section.

"No, I don't think that would work, Dick," said Walt. "Those guys don't work that way."

"They don't care about timing," said Huemer, meaning, apparently, that composers with the background of a Stravinsky would not be aware of the timing problems that an animator faces in fitting visible action to music.

"They are of another school," said Disney. "We are developing an entirely different school right here in this place. . . ."

By the close of the meeting, Walt Disney had definitely decided to use some music other than Pierné's *Cydalise* for the Greek mythology number that he was beginning to like very much.

"Let's do some exploring first," he said. "Let's see if we can't put together the right stuff."

But he warned that if they couldn't find music with "the right class," he would have to delay work on the mythology section.

By the following February, a storyman named George Stallings had typed up a brief continuity for the third, fourth, and fifth movements of *The Pastoral Symphony*. It contained suggestions for some of the most effective animated images in the finished work. There is the "thunderous dancing by Bacchus which stimulates the build-up into a flurry of wild frolicking. Centaurs and Girls [not yet "centaurettes"] dancing about with much vim and gusto."

It seems a pity that Disney didn't commission an original composition to accompany his mythological ballet, as Diaghilev would have. The picturization of characters and incidents from Greek mythology has attracted artists from Titian to Picasso, and includes many themes that are particularly well suited to animated drawing,

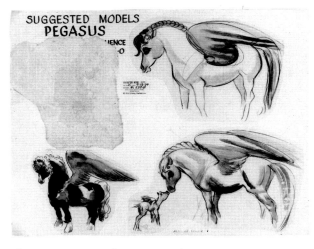

Suggested models for Pegasus. *Some images created for* Fantasia *looked better as inspirational sketches than when animated on the screen. Not so the flying horses. Artists have been trying to represent them since at least the early 5th century* B.C., *when Etruscans created the polychromed terra-cotta revetment in the form of a winged horse that is in the Vatican Museums. But a flying horse cries out for animation.*

The Pegasus family circles down and out of the clouds
in a scene animated by Don Towsley and laid out
by Ken Anderson (above). The flying horses circle an
island crowned with a peristyle and come in for a landing
on an Elysian lake in a scene animated by Towsley and
Harry Hamsel and laid out by Anderson (opposite).

*Centaur sketches originally drawn for Pierné's* Cydalise *were retained for* The Pastoral Symphony, *but the Studio gave the female centaurs a new name with a 1930s flavor—centaurettes (opposite, above). The search for female figures for the* Pastoral *also resulted in a poetic watercolor by R. C. Cormack—but the water nymphs he pictured never reached the screen (opposite, below).*

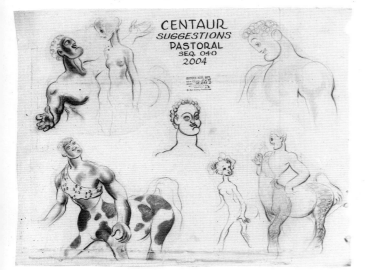

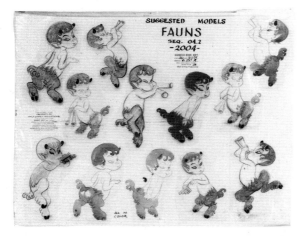

but the subject deserved an original score tailored to its musical and rhythmic requirements as well.

We find Pegasus on a vase made in the fourth century B.C., and he has appeared in many paintings since, but the Disney artists were the first to depict winged horses actually flying—theirs was the problem of showing whether such beasts landed front legs first, or hind legs first, and how their powerful wings might have moved.

Forty years later, Ray Harryhausen, the leading animator of three-dimensional models, put a flying horse into his 1981 M-G-M film *Clash of the Titans*, and he acknowledged his debt to Disney. "The question with Pegasus was: What do you do with four legs when you have glorious wings to keep you up? I thought of Disney's *Fantasia* instantly, and in my early experiments, I tried to animate graceful horses with their languid legs making beautiful designs in the air—and it just didn't work. . . . A cartoon animator, moving stylized characters against stylized backgrounds, has much more flexibility." In *The Pastoral Symphony*, this flexibility resulted in animation by Eric Larson, Don Towsley, and others that flows well and has, for the most part, a pleasing, rhythmic pattern.

Disney had experimented with the animation of the faun since his 1930 Silly Symphony *Playful Pan*. In *The Pastoral Symphony*, animator Walt Kelly, who was later to achieve fame as the creator of the comic strip *Pogo*, animated fauns with the tail and hind legs of a goat, small horns, and pointed ears. In the paintings of Pinturicchio and others, the faun is shown playing the syrinx, or pipes of pan. In the animation of Disney, the fauns frisk, goatlike, while piping like humans, as they might in our fantasies.

The centaurs are *Fantasia*'s nadir. Master animator Eric Larson, who did not work on them, says that "they were not pleasing forms to begin with, and they seemed clumsy in action." The great animator Bill Tytla has evaluated Winsor McCay's *The Centaurs* (1916), and *Captain Grogg Among Other Strange Creatures* (1920) by the Swedish animator Victor Bergdahl. Tytla was of the opinion that both these films had centaurs superior in design, draftsmanship, and animation to the centaurs in *The Pastoral Symphony*.

"I remember how badly I wanted to do them at that time," said Tytla. "Then I got a call from Walt and he wanted me to do *Night on Bald Mountain*. When I saw the centaurs in the picture, they looked gutless. They should have been big stallions with dark, Mediterranean faces on them. Instead they were castrated horsies with a type of Anglo-Saxon head. I was a polo player. I like to be around horses. I could have done good things with them."

"It's whatcha do with whatcha got," Disney frequently said. He apparently believed that *Fantasia* needed Tytla's artistry more for animating the devil on Bald Mountain, and he was certainly right, for that is *Fantasia*'s highest peak. Yet Tytla may have been the only artist on Disney's staff capable of both drawing and animating the centaurs as they should have been done. Freddy Moore consistently created charming and appealing animation, but he was miscast as animation supervisor of the symphony's second movement, the one in which centaurs romance centaurettes. Both centaurs and cen-

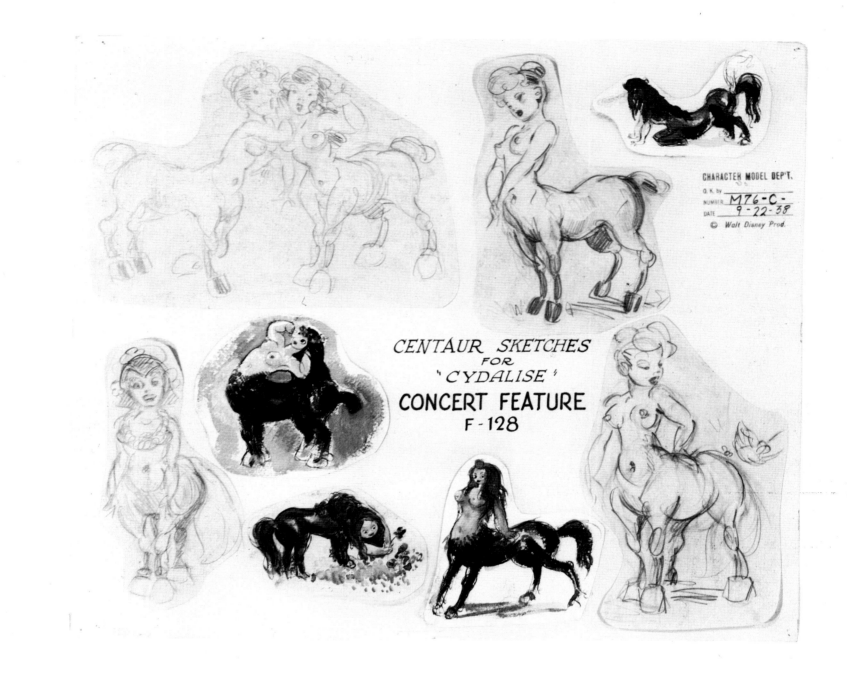

CENTAUR SKETCHES
FOR
'CYDALISE'
CONCERT FEATURE
F-128

CHARACTER MODEL DEP'T.
O.K. by
NUMBER M76-C-
DATE 9-22-38
© Walt Disney Prod.

The exploration of themes for the mythological section
produced some interesting preliminary artwork (above),
but the females degenerated into saccharine girls (right).

taurettes moved clumsily at times, and the centaurs were sometimes effeminate in their movements.

The centaurettes presented another problem. As drawn, they didn't fit an ancient Greek and/or mythological setting. Their upper torsos belonged to what was known around the Disney Studio as "Freddy Moore girls," typically American nubile adolescents who are now called "Lolitas" in honor of the eponymous heroine of Nabokov's famous novel. The lower torsos were horses.

Moore and his former assistant, Oliver M. Johnston, Jr., drew and animated the girl part easily and well. As no less an authority than the great British caricaturist Sir David Low remarked, "Compare the play of human expression in the face of Snow White with that in the faces of the centaurettes in *Fantasia* and mark the striking improvement. Subtlety is now possible." This subtlety of expression is best seen in the centaurette fashion show, as when a centaurette tries on two doves for a hat, in an attempt to please cupid. But the girls look as out of place on Mount Olympus as Lana Turner would have looked playing Greek comedy. The "Freddy Moore girls" belong in an American high school setting — which is how they are used later to good effect, when they dance to Benny Goodman's recording of *All the Cats Join In* in Disney's 1946 pop cartoon *Make Mine Music*.

The winged cupids, who pipe an entranced centaur into a romance with a centaurette, also give us a picture of the way Disney solved problems at the time *Fantasia* was in production. "One day Otto Englander burst into Walt's office with an idea for ending the first movement of *The Pastoral Symphony*. . . . Englander found Walt seated on the floor of his office amid a clutter of chromium tubes and blue leatherette cushions. Walt explained sheepishly that he was considering a new design for an animator's chair, and he was taking it apart to see how it was constructed. Walt listened as Englander explained his idea . . . approved it, and returned to his dissection of the chair." Bob Thomas, Disney's biographer, tells this anecdote.

Englander's idea was to have the three cupids who have brought the centaur and the centaurette together draw a curtain on their activities. As it now appears on the screen, two of the cupids fly off; the last one looks to the right, then to the left, and flies over to part the curtains and peek inside. Cupid as a naked, winged baby boy with a rosy bottom has been an artistic convention at least since Cupid held a mirror for Venus in Velásquez's seventeenth-century masterpiece *The Toilet of Venus*. But this being animation, his rosy bottom metamorphoses into a heart to symbolize the love scene that he is witnessing.

The third movement, *Bacchanal* in the Disney version, is the country dance that Beethoven wrote for the scherzo. It is performed with gusto by fauns and cupids, centaurs and centaurettes, frolicking in a harvest festival in honor of Bacchus, god of the vine.

Disney's Bacchus is not the curly-haired youth of Roman art, but a fat and tipsy wine god who rides his unicorn-jackass with a rollicking movement that is the essence of drunken revelry. Ward Kimball was the animation supervisor of the Bacchanalian bits, and they have Kimball's freewheeling zest. When the donkey swallows

A sequence of inspirational sketches shows a cupid on a pedestal drawing the attention of his fellows to a lonely centaur and a lonely centaurette—a situation that causes all the cupids to converge, like figures on a Valentine (opposite, above). In a frame from the film (opposite, below), three piping cupids, animated by Milt Neil, coax the offscreen centaurette into her meeting with the lonely centaur.

When Walt Disney looked at inspirational sketches of fauns, unicorns, winged horses, centaurs, and centaurettes such as these, he mused aloud: "I believe you should start with one thing—like the little fauns, and keep topping each section with some new surprise," he said. "There's terrific interest in the beginning in these little fauns . . . the flutes you hear is the way they play their pipes. . . . At the most, it's 150 feet, or something like that, where you

get over your opening. . . . And let it have a slow
tempo, so far as business *happening;* I don't mean the
tempo of the music.

"But don't give away anything," Walt added—
meaning not to picture the love interest as centaurettes
right away. "You want that as an additional surprise."
And then, hearing a little dance rhythm in the
music, Walt pantomimed fauns for his story staff,
using his hands as horns.

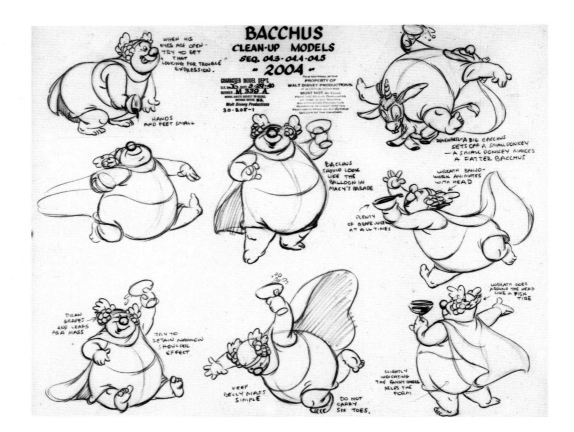

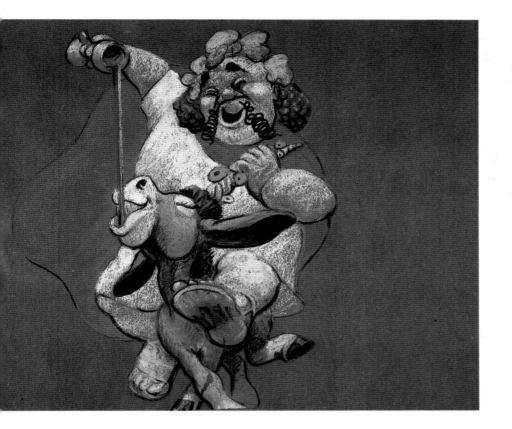

Fantasia's *low point* was its characterizations of Bacchus, centaurs, and centaurettes as visualizations of *The Pastoral Symphony. Perhaps the fault lay not in the concept but in the inability of Disney's artists to capture in line drawings the gutsy ethnic look of the Character Model Department's pastel suggestions (rendered on "toothy" brown paper to emphasize the roughness of the chalk). The sheet of Bacchus clean-up models (opposite, above) shows the ultimate form in which the wine god reached the screen. When Joe Grant okayed the 3/29/40 model sheet that said, "Bacchus should look like the balloon in Macy's parade," the Studio moved away from the bold design of the original concept toward a balloon-like character who did indeed owe more to Macy's Thanksgiving Day Parade than to Greek mythology. The rollicking animation of Bacchus, by Ward Kimball, Walt Kelly, and others, was a marvel of sly accents; the final model design was a misfortune.*

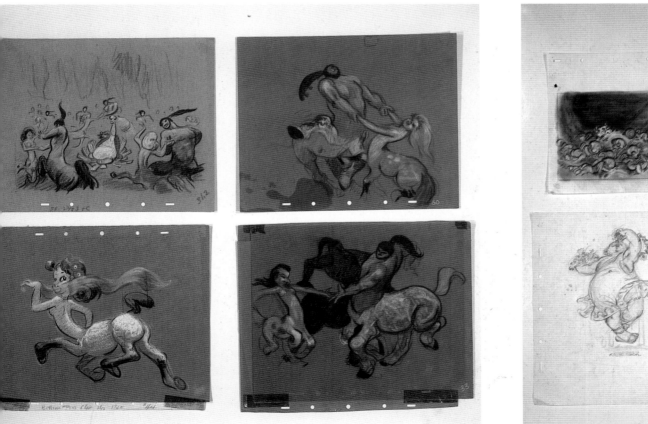

It took a while for Joe Grant and his staff to visualize just how a god throws a lightning bolt. In the early version (above), one god fires a bolt from a bow, while another simply drops a lightning bomb through a rent in the clouds. By December, 1939, the lightning-thrower had evolved into Zeus (opposite), and in these two model sheets he hurls lightning bolts like a baseball pitcher uncorking his best fastball.

wine, then smacks his lips and hiccups, that is pure Kimball. We can also see the animation of Walt Kelly, a member of the Kimball unit, in his section.

The storm with which Beethoven interrupted his jolly gathering of country folk is interpreted by the Disney artists as a storm made by Vulcan, blacksmith of the gods, who forges giant thunderbolts for Zeus to throw. Of the five parts of *The Pastoral Symphony*, this fourth movement, codirected by Ham Luske and Jim Handley, with art direction by Ken Anderson, is most successful at expressing Beethoven's music in animated images.

Zeus and Vulcan are very well animated by Art Babbitt, though they are not beautifully drawn. To compare the original character designs, or even the storyboard sketches, with Babbitt's animation is to see that his background as a cartoonist had ill-prepared him to draw human figures of classical proportions. Babbitt said that when he got the assignment from Disney, he took a crash course in drawing the human figure under Don Graham at the Disney training school. It was not enough. The face of Babbitt's Vulcan is a cartoon convention, right to his cherry nose; and the Art Deco design of

SUGGESTIONS FOR ZEUS
PASTORAL
SEQ. 04-4
2004

Zeus, complete with scalloped beard, often loses its strength in animation. The movement, however, has the qualities that always distinguish Babbitt's animation: the weight and rhythmic timing in Vulcan's resounding hammer blows; the surprising use of a commonplace action carefully analyzed as Zeus yawns, kicks off both his slippers, and pulls clouds over himself as if they were bedclothes after he has tossed away his last lightning bolt. Vulcan at his forge has been pictured by such artists as Bruegel the Elder; Vulcan in action, hammering at his forge, had to wait for the artists of the Disney Studio.

In the days when *Fantasia* was being made, whole sequences would be color-keyed, scene by scene, so that the colors in each shot would harmonize, not only with each other, but with the colors in the preceding and following shots; and would be keyed as well to the changes in the emotions being expressed by the actions. "Before the narrative pattern was completed in any great detail," wrote Harvard professor Robert D. Feild in his seminal 1942 study, *The Art of Walt Disney,* "an overall color scheme was worked out in sympathy with the general mood of the music and patterned to correspond with the development of the subject matter." Ken Anderson,

150

The Character Model Department designed a Vulcan, god of fire, to hammer out the bolts on his forge. Apollo, god of light, was pictured driving his fiery chariot to the horizon, while another artist explored his driving technique—reins for three horses in his left hand, whip in his right.

Vulcan holds a lightning bolt up in the air (above). Art Babbitt animated Vulcan, and though his cartoony, lump-nosed god failed to capture the passion of the Character Model Department's conception, Vulcan's movements had the weight and rhythmic timing that always distinguish Babbitt's animation. Effects artist Josh Meador gave the lightning bolt its glow, the forge its sparks. At right, a comparison of a frame from the film with an inspirational painting of Zeus shows a similar loss of integrity of design but a gain in dynamic action.

Several backgrounds of Mount Olympus with the
Elysian Fields were painted for The Pastoral
Symphony. The frame opposite is from the sunset in
the fifth movement crowned by the moon and
stars at night. All the scenes retain the basic feeling of
the cloud-covered mountain in the painting (above),
which hangs today in the office of Ron Miller, president
and chief executive officer of Walt Disney Productions.
The backgrounds for The Pastoral Symphony were
mainly the work of six artists: Claude Coats, Ray
Huffine, W. Richard Anthony, Arthur Riley, Gerald
Nevius, and Roy Forkum, who is shown opposite.
In animation, the layout artist establishes the field
of action and outlines the appearance of the "set," but
the background artist must make it visually attractive.

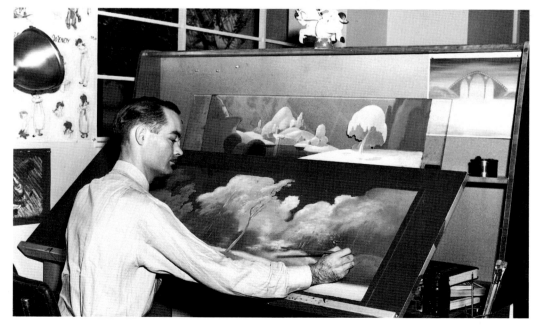

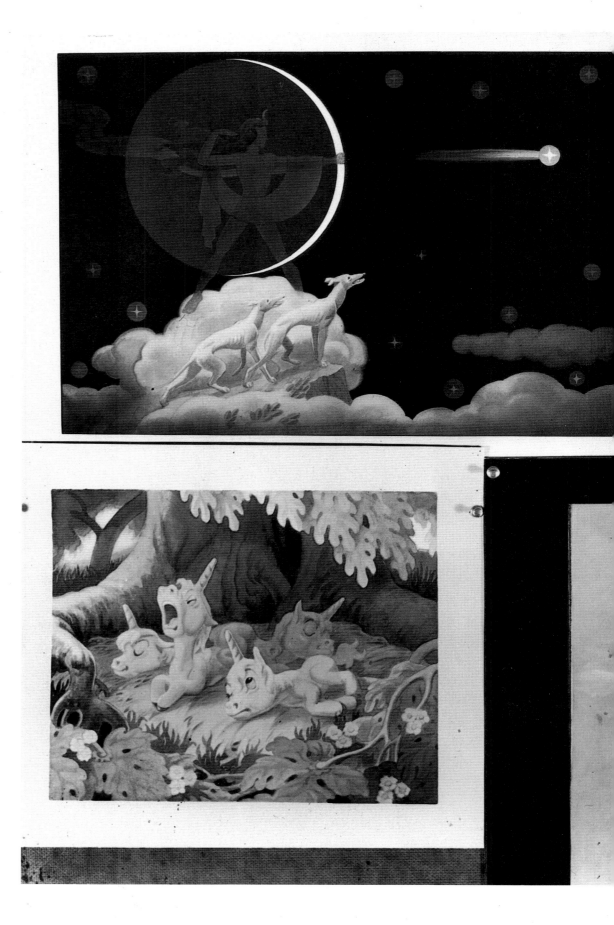

These inspirational sketches of Diana, the unicorns, a centaur and centaurette watching the rainbow goddess Iris, and Apollo driving his fiery chariot were the first versions of the characters that Walt saw. His suggestions and comments shaped their ultimate appearance on the screen.

"Morpheus, Thou knowest hym wel, the god of slep," wrote Chaucer, nearly 500 years before Fantasia. But it wasn't until the advent of animation that artists could actually show Morpheus (opposite, above)— metamorphosed as a lovely, dark-haired woman— bringing in the night sky while crossing the horizon. Jack Campbell animated the figure while George Rowley was responsible for the drapery, making the folds of the great purple cloak cover the Elysian Fields, "so that," as Deems Taylor later described it, "the afterglow merged into twilight, and the twilight into darkness." Iris, the rainbow goddess, travels across the sky trailing the rainbow after her (above). Campbell, who animated key scenes involving Snow White and the Blue Fairy, animated this female goddess. Rowley animated the effects of the air-brushed rainbow and its reflection as it travels over water from the horizon. For the storm in the fourth movement, Cornett Wood animated two wind gods (opposite, below) progressing across the screen from left to right, blowing up a windstorm.

the art director who color-keyed the storm in *The Pastoral Symphony,*
painted a color scheme chart that was designed to show the background painters what colors they should use to express Bacchus's
fear as he gets lightning bolts thrown at him, or the relief of the
characters emerging from shelter after the storm.

The formalized landscapes for *The Pastoral Symphony*
were the boldest yet seen in an animated feature. "Disney was the
first to realize," wrote Lewis Jacobs, "that color in motion pictures
need not bear any resemblance to color in real life, that objects on
the screen could be endowed with any pigmentation dictated by the
imagination." Forms could be suggested rather than realistically presented. The texture of the paint itself could be used to express the
texture of the object painted. In Disney's Arcadia, the leaves of a tree
could be (and were) boysenberry as easily as green. All that was
necessary was that those who saw them should say (or at least feel):
"I, too, have lived in Arcadia."

Indeed, the way that *The Pastoral Symphony* got boysenberry trees, as reported in the Disney Studio house organ, shows how
deliciously experimental *Fantasia* really was:

"Baffled in his search for a new and different color for a
Hugh Hennesy layout, and having tried everything on the palette,
[Ray] Huffine sulked in his room during the lunch hour. In the course
of [going through] a home-packed lunch which contained, among other
items, a jar of Mrs. Huffine's best boysenberry jam, Huffine is reported to have done a classic double take, then to have reached for
the jar and laid a delicate boysenberry wash over the background.
Results were startlingly satisfactory, and, disguised as a background, Mrs. Huffine's boysenberry premiered middle of the week
in New York."

*Shepherd's Hymn of Thanksgiving After the Storm, Allegretto,* was the designation Beethoven gave to the fifth and last movement of his *Pastoral Symphony.* This movement was used by Disney
for the animation of a sunset after the storm in which a number of
Greek gods are brought to life to perform their most characteristic
actions. The artists at the Disney Studio used the paints on their
palettes in consonance with the colors of Beethoven's musical tones.
What they came up with was the fulfillment of Disney's enthusiastic
cry when he first saw three-strip Technicolor back in 1932: "At last!
We can show a rainbow on the screen!"

Apollo, the god of light, drives his fiery chariot, drawn by
three golden horses, the embodiment of the setting sun, in an image
as memorable as the castle in the setting sun in *Snow White.*

"You know, fellows," said Disney, in urging his artists to
make that sun shine, "this will probably be the first and last time
the public is ever going to see the sun. So let 'em have it. Burn up
the screen with that color."

It is in *The Pastoral Symphony* more than in any other of
his works that Disney's reach exceeds his grasp; and yet, what he is
grasping at is the basic right of animation as the youngest of the arts:
the right to treat of the great mythological themes which have attracted artists from the anonymous painters of antiquity to Picasso.

*Two would-be seducers in the great hall of Duke Alvise, their capes flaring up behind them, ready for action.*

# THE HOURS

**D**ance of the Hours, a ballet in the opera *La Gioconda (The Smiling One)* by Amilcare Ponchielli, was first performed at La Scala Opera House in Milan, in April, 1876.

In *Fantasia, Dance of the Hours* is used for an animal ballet that burlesques the classical ballet of graceful ballerinas and noble male dancers. Ponchielli wrote the music to express a pageant of the hours of the day, and Disney makes that the form of his film. It is divided into four parts:

*Ostrich Ballet; Morning.* We see elegant wrought iron gates. They open and we move down a hall toward diaphanous white curtains. They part to disclose a ballerina asleep at the top of a stairway. She wakens, stretches, and rises. She is an ostrich. With excruciating grace she pirouettes over to other sleeping ostriches, whom she awakens. Taking up a cornucopia, she throws fruit to the members of the ensemble, who swallow it whole. Oranges, bananas, and pineapples make interesting shapes in their ostrich necks. When the dancers attempt to take a bunch of grapes away from the prima ballerina, she flees, and they chase her outdoors to the pool.

*Hippo Ballet; Afternoon.* The prima ballerina is a hippopotamus named Hyacinth. Waking in her pool, she powders her nose and under her arms and admires herself in a mirror. Her vanity reassured, she casts the powder puff aside and is helped out of the pool by two chorus hippos. Then Hyacinth Hippo goes into her solo dance. The exertion causes her to yawn greatly, rub her eyes, stretch, droop, and fall into the arms of the chorus hippos, who escort her back to her couch and restful slumber.

*Elephant Ballet; Evening.* Elephants appear in evening attire. They go to the pool and blow large pink bubbles, with which they perform a bubble dance. In time, the bubbles stack up under the sleeping hippo's couch. The wind rises, carrying bubble-borne elephants and hippos out of the garden. The bubbles have also borne aloft the couch of Hyacinth Hippo, but now the couch spirals back to earth, the bubbles blow away, and Hyacinth is left alone, still sleeping, as night falls.

*Alligator Ballet; Night.* Yellow eyes peer out of the darkness, watching Hyacinth sleep. A backlight snaps on, revealing alligators. They slide down columns and slither over to Hyacinth, heads snapping, tails twisting—when suddenly their leader appears. He is Ben Ali Gator, and he is dressed, like the others, in a black cape lined with red, but his cocky walk says that he is boss. Bending over Hyacinth, he leers; she wakes; they go into their dance. It is a spectacular adagio, an amorous *pas de deux*, which suddenly erupts into the wildest pursuit of everybody by everybody in the history of ballet. Alligators and hippos play hide-and-seek around marble columns; alligators ride ostriches; an elephant rides an alligator; alligators spin elephants overhead; hippos whirl alligators around by their tails. Ben Ali Gator spins Hyacinth Hippo and, on a musical accent, throws her down, assuming a triumphant posture over her. The camera trucks back quickly through the hall where we came in. The gates slam violently and fall off their hinges.

B en Ali Gator was born in a conference room at the old Walt Disney Studio on Hyperion Avenue in Los Angeles Monday, October 17, 1938, sometime between the hours of 11:00 A.M. and 12:30 P.M.

At that very first story meeting, Walt pretty well outlined *Dance of the Hours.*

"Don't you think we might work it this way," he asked his story staff as the meeting drew to a close. "Dawn is the ostrich; Day would be, say, the hippos; Evening, the elephants; Night, the crocodiles. Then when they chase off the Hours of the Night, let them all come in because that's the finale." Many changes were made to *Dance of the Hours* as it progressed from story through direction, layout, and animation; but that remained the clear, simple form of the thing.

By the time Walt Disney started to plan a comedy of gags to Ponchielli's *Dance of the Hours,* he had been putting gags in cartoons for eighteen years, beginning with the one-minute films he made for the Kansas City Film Ad company in 1920. By 1938, he had produced dozens of the funniest films ever made—who could forget Pluto tangled up with flypaper in *Playful Pluto,* Mickey Mouse conducting in a cyclone in *The Band Concert,* or Donald Duck dealing with a recalcitrant mainspring in *Clock Cleaners?* And now Walt was doing a burlesque of the ballet in which the dancers were ostriches, elephants, and hippos.

"Let's take these animals, screwy as they are," he said at that story conference, "and stage this all as legitimate, and done as a perfect ballet. . . . Later, then, let the slips come, rather than in the beginning."

Joe Grant got his point. "Don't be blinded by gags."

"The whole incongruity of the thing," said Walt, "is the elephants and hippos doing what graceful people do. Of course, they can use natural props like their trunks."

For an hour and a half the story crew listened to the record of *Dance of the Hours.* And everywhere in its overfamiliar score, Walt heard ideas for comedy.

Walt said that they could leave it to Deems Taylor to tip off the audience to the ballet's scenario in his spoken introduction, and Deems did, saying, "It's a pageant of the hours of the day. All this takes place in the great hall—with the garden beyond—of the Palace of Duke Alvise, a Venetian nobleman."

"Seems like this is the Evening Hours to me," said Walt as he listened to one passage in the music. "Here's the slinking hours. Shadowy . . . seems like the hours of blackness should be something like—*alligators.*"

"Something that has flash—very funny expressions," added Joe Grant, apparently trying to keep their options open, but Walt was already seeing alligators very vividly.

"When the music goes DI DUMP!" Walt said, "they open their mouths slowly, like alligators do."

A chiming was heard in the music.

"Here's more clock," said Stuart Buchanan, a storyman who has attained his measure of immortality as the voice of the Huntsman in *Snow White.*

"I would like to see this ballet really symbolize something," said Walt, "because that would make it twice as effective . . . here come the hours chasing the others away."

And here the stenographer records that Walt burst into song, singing along with the record, in one of those uninhibited moments that few but his story people ever saw. ("God, he was great at pantomime, at acting out what he wanted," Dick Huemer recalled. "Funny as Chaplin when he got going.")

On this day, Walt was going great, and the stenographer records his decision to use alligators in *Dance of the Hours* with these words: "Here's the funny part where the guys go . . . (Walt bares his teeth, snarls . . . prances.) Slinky alligators would be swell, I think." What Walt thought has become a classic.

As caricature of movement as well as pose, as the perfection of the comedy of gags, and as a triumph of the layout man's art, *Dance of the Hours* is a milestone in the history of film. Through the story conference notes and the recollections of artists who worked on it, we can trace its evolution from Walt Disney's hearing alligators in a few bars of Ponchielli to its ultimate caricature of the romantic ballet, a masterpiece of comic animation that extends the meaning of caricature.

"The comic does not exist outside the pale of what is strictly human," observed the French philosopher Henri Bergson, in his celebrated essay *Laughter*. "You may laugh at an animal, but only because you have detected in it some human attitude or expression."

Walt was always on the lookout for the human attitude that could be caricatured in terms of something that wasn't human.

"Anybody looking at this now can see caricature in it," he said, looking at sketches of Hyacinth Hippo. "I like touches like at the end where she pulls her skirt down and it's no good, it won't stay. You know what might be funny when she sits up and sees him? The old gag they always use where the girl pulls her covers up—takes whatever she has and holds it in front of her—and the hippo pulls her skirt up and she has nothing down below. They still do that—you see it in pictures where people bust into bedrooms."

And the gag was sketched up, and animated, so that, on the screen, when we see Hyacinth Hippo, prima ballerina and unquenchable coquette, surprised while napping by the lustful Ben Ali Gator, she quickly covers her naked chest with her transparent tutu, leaving the rest of her bare.

Walt seemed to see endless possibilities in Ben Ali Gator.

"I don't know yet how we'll stage this, but I see a lot of steps, and jumping off platforms," he said, while looking at story sketches of alligators (which they all interchangeably called crocodiles). "That crocodile won't come in like he does here, he would appear up on a high thing and [with] that 'Hah!' sort of hissing, and leap out on the floor. And as he sneaks up to her [Hyacinth Hippo] I see him go right down into a regular crocodile for a while, and then come up into the human. And there's one thing we could do on some of this spinning— they've got big stomachs—they could darn near go into a thing where they spin on their stomachs."

John Lounsbery shows Leopold Stokowski the view from the animator's chair (above). Lounsbery has several drawings of Ben Ali Gator in slightly different positions registered on pegs at the bottom of his light board. Flipping the drawings gives him an impression of how the movement will come alive on the screen. He consults the model sheet of Ben Ali above the light board to maintain consistent design. The exposure sheet at his right shows the number of 35mm frames of film allotted to action in the scene. The result (opposite, below) is Ben Ali Gator smitten. The lusty alligator leers behind his hand at the sleeping Hyacinth Hippo in an inspirational sketch (opposite, above). When the animator took over the character he awakened love in the alligator's savage breast—and captured the moment by having Ben Ali crawl behind Hyacinth's couch, pop his head up in quick looks, then go into this famous love-smitten pose.

"We're caricature," said Walt Disney at another story conference. Indeed, he called his animated films "a caricature of life," and he explained, "Animation is different from the other arts. Its language is the language of caricature. Our most difficult job was to develop the cartoon's unnatural but seemingly natural anatomy for humans and animals."

Throughout the production of *Dance of the Hours,* Disney kept trying to make clearer to his artists what he meant by caricature in animation. When Hyacinth Hippo is observed, Venuslike, at her toilette, she is a presentation of human vanity whose point is made sharper by its distortion.

The salient feature of the romantic ballet has been described by the great choreographer George Balanchine as the "elfin, unattainable heroines and heroes who aimed at—and so seldom secured—permanent happiness." The illusions of all the overweight and overeager, who would be elfin and initially unattainable, are more swiftly punctured when ballerinas are shown as hippos in tutus. Even static caricatures could accomplish this to some extent. The tradition of caricaturing human aspirations with animal analogies stretches from Grandville and Tenniel to T. S. Sullivant and Heinrich Kley. It is a tradition that Disney artists had been consciously studying since the early thirties. Employing heroines who are hippos, elephants, and ostriches, and heroes who are alligators, to caricature the strictly human pursuit of happiness lies squarely in that tradition.

But *Dance of the Hours,* with its animated exaggerations, does more. "This is definitely ballet, a caricature of a ballet," said Disney. It is a caricature of the ballet in which not only the subject, temper, and mood of the romantic ballet are parodied, but the basic vocabulary of steps and movements as well.

"To the dance," wrote the great Russian animator Alexandre Alexeieff, "animation brings weightlessness and an unlimited metamorphosis." When a human being executes the *grand jeté,* this "big leap" is the triumphant achievement of the illusion of weightlessness. When a hippopotamus does the same thing, it is a caricature of that illusion. When Hyacinth Hippo flies, sylphlike, to the arms of Ben Ali Gator, she flattens him—despite the precaution that animator Norman Tate took of having Ali brace himself with his tail. Only an art of movement could lampoon the triumph of grace over gravity that is the essence of ballet—so the basic joke in *Dance of the Hours* is based on the nature of the animation medium itself.

The joke was told so well because *Dance of the Hours* was codirected by two keen caricaturists, Norman Ferguson and T. Hee.

"Fergy," who also animated the scenes in which Hyacinth powders her nose and goes into her dance, was the actual creator of Disney's Pluto, the mute pup who was such a cunning caricature of the human adolescent. And Hee, whose given name of Thornton underwent a comic abbreviation ideal for cartoon credits, was originally hired by Disney for his skill as a caricaturist when Walt decided to burlesque film stars as nursery rhyme characters in *Mother Goose Goes Hollywood* (1938).

Walt immediately recognized T. Hee as multitalented—an-

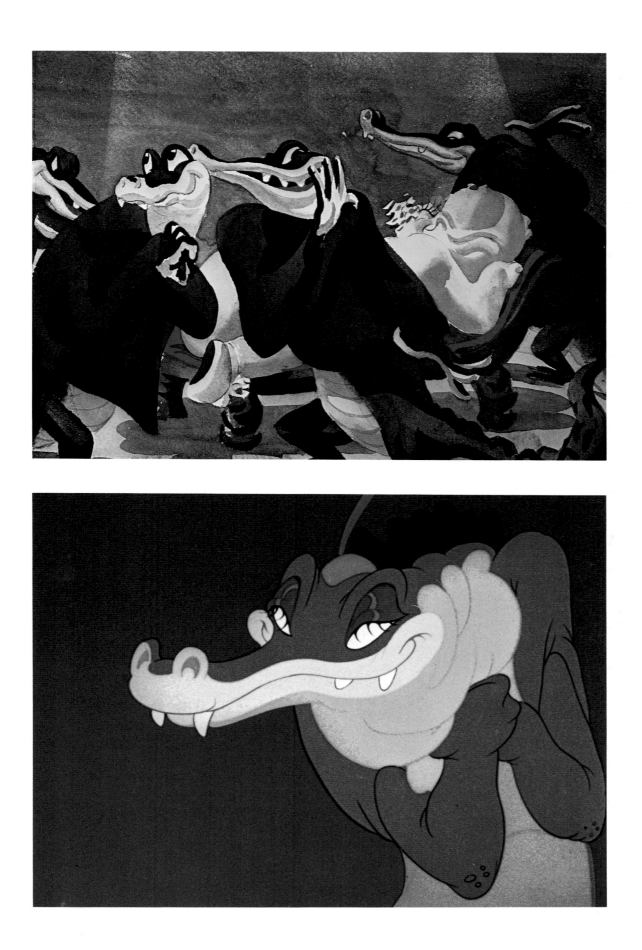

*Norman Ferguson, who co-directed* Dance of the
Hours *with T. Hee, shows a painted cel of Mlle.
Upanova, the ostrich ballerina, to Deems Taylor (above).
A caricature of Kendall O'Connor (opposite)—he was
an art director on* Snow White, Pinocchio, *and* Dumbo
*and the layout artist for* Dance of the Hours, *who
with Ferguson was a master of imaginative staging.*

other example of what Stokowski saw as Disney's "ability to find and
attract highly talented designers in form and color," his "instinct for
perceiving great gifts in young artists" that reminded Stokowski of
Diaghilev.

*Pinocchio, Fantasia,* and *Bambi* were all being worked on
at the same time from 1938 to 1940, and Disney first assigned T.
Hee to work on *Pinocchio,* originally as a storyman, drawing pictures,
writing dialogue, and acting out scenes. Then he made him a director
on *Pinocchio* scenes involving the fox, the cat, and Stromboli. Bill
Tytla, who animated Stromboli, had the 260-pound T. Hee dress up
like the gargantuan puppet master and act out his movements.

On *Fantasia,* not surprisingly, Disney assigned T. Hee to
*Dance of the Hours.* Some of the dancers were to be elephants and,
as layout man Kendall O'Connor later commented: "Remembering
our efforts to establish elephantine character, I feel we owe an ev-
erlasting debt of gratitude to Tee's predilection for baggy pants."

"That hip action is swell," said Walt at one of the story meetings as he looked at live action of human dancers performing *Dance
of the Hours* while imagining that they were elephants. "Get those
hips moving back and forth, plenty of rear views—elephants have a
baggy-pants effect."

But in addition to his flair for baggy-pants comedy, T. Hee
was a subtle artist with definite ideas about the action he wanted to
distort. The basic idea of the ballet in the opera was not being
changed, it was being amusingly broadened.

"Ballet, of course, is an abstraction, in the way of movement, of story telling," T. Hee explained. "*Dance of the Hours* tried
to tell the story of morning, noon, and night—and night is a time of
revelry, when everything breaks down. If you just take it a little bit
further, it becomes a satire. Chaplin often said that he walked a
tightrope with comedy on one side and tragedy on the other; if he
tipped to one side, it would be tragedy; if he tipped to the other side,
it would be comedy. This was the kind of thing I was thinking of when
we were doing this: that this would be comedy, because we could lean
it just a little to the comedy side—you know, with these guys chasing
the dames around, it was as though they were going to get somebody.
But nobody ever got anybody."

T. Hee followed Walt's concept of taking the title literally
and making the segment an actual dance of the hours, by following
the movement of light through space and time. The idea would be to
show the first group of dancers in costumes colored to suggest the
delicate light of dawn. Then a second group would enter, dressed to
represent the brilliant light of noonday. As these withdrew, a third
group would enter, dressed in the tones of early evening. And, finally,
there would be characters dressed in the black of night.

The duties of the layout man were defined by the Studio
very precisely: "The layout artist plans the exact size of each scene,
general color schemes, and all working details of the background and
characters. He is responsible for the plan of action that the animator
follows in relation to the background and the music. Hence, he must
understand action and be able to give the animator characters that
work and scenes in which action is possible."

166

No layout man fills that bill better than Ken O'Connor, who laid out many of the scenes under T. Hee's direction for the animators of *Dance of the Hours.*

The layout man begins his work by making thumbnail sketches of how the scenes will be staged. "You know," T. Hee said, "this thing was so beautifully detailed in thumbnail sketches, that you could look at them and see the whole picture unfold. If we never did any animation, we knew exactly what was going to happen."

After the layout man makes the thumbnail sketches, he creates a rough layout. "Prior to rough layout," wrote O'Connor about *Dance of the Hours,* "we adopted a linear motif for each sequence. In the first sequence our motif was vertical and horizontal in design. This tied in with the vertical necks and legs of the ostriches, and as far as possible, the birds were kept moving horizontally and vertically. It also expressed the static calm of early morning hours, which was further emphasized by cool grayed colors in the backgrounds and neutrals in the characters."

"We figured that these ostriches were really verticals," said T. Hee, "in the way that they pointed their toes for example. All their movements were sort of like this, so we had a high horizon line."

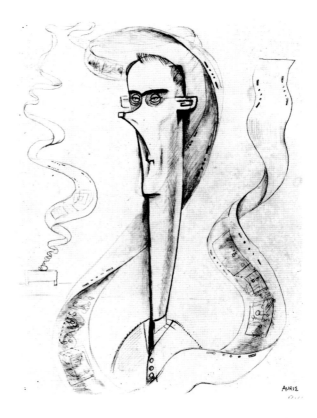

"In the second sequence," wrote O'Connor, "we suddenly moved outdoors into the brilliant light of noon. Here we adapted the ellipse as a motif. This was more active than the previous one and tied in with the rotund hippos and their circular ballet movements.

"Our third sequence motif was the still more active movement of the serpentine line," O'Connor continued.

"The elephants carried out the serpentine movement," T. Hee explained. "We changed the horizon line to a low eye level and all the elephants were above the horizon line. Their big bodies moved back and forth swayingly, and their trunks undulatingly. We went to evening colors in the backgrounds—lavenders and blues—so that it would be like twilight."

"For the fourth sequence, involving the crocodiles, we introduced a zigzag motif as being the most violent," explained O'Connor. "It was related to the angular reptilian construction and carried out by diagonal paths of action."

And now the key concept of the art of caricature in motion came into play.

The strength of a Disney caricature lies in the subtle similarities its movements reveal between human beings on the one hand and animals, plants, and even inanimate objects on the other. In each case, the artists look for real characteristics of movement to exaggerate, so that, for example, the predatory nature of an animal such as an alligator humorously overstates the idea of a predatory human male, a Don Juan on the prowl.

The design of the alligators and elephants in *Dance of the Hours* is based on the alligators and elephants of Heinrich Kley, just as the design of the hippos and ostriches is based, in part, on the designs of T. S. Sullivant. In his drive for "an expanded capability of fitting a variety of styles to a variety of stories in many moods," Walt Disney assembled in the 1930s one of the largest collections of Kley's

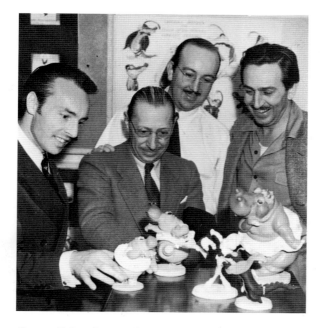

George Balanchine and Igor Stravinsky are shown three-dimensional models of Hyacinth Hippo by T. Hee and Walt Disney (above). On the wall are the model sheets of Ben Ali Gator that John Lounsbery is using in the picture on page 164. The inspirational painting of Ben Ali Gator (opposite) is by Lee Blair, a talented painter who worked as a storyman on Fantasia, an animator on Bambi, and an art supervisor on Saludos Amigos.

drawings in existence, and he also insisted that his artists study models that ranged from Sir John Tenniel, illustrator of *Alice in Wonderland,* to Ernest Shepard, who made the simple but eloquent drawings for *Winnie the Pooh.*

But it was necessary for Disney artists to redesign these static caricatures into shapes that could be animated. Albert Hurter, the Swiss-born sketch artist whose inspirational sketches gave many Silly Symphonies and much of *Snow White* and *Pinocchio* their style and appearance, adapted the Sullivant hippo to a cartoon character. Campbell Grant provided a model sheet for the ostrich dancers and Martin Provensen, who, with his wife, Alice, later became a leading illustrator of children's books, posed elephant ballerinas with iridescent bubbles big as beach balls. James Bodrero contributed to the character design, as did Earl Hurd. (*There* was an example of the continuity of animation history, for it was Hurd who invented the very process of cel animation back in 1914!)

For animators who liked to see three-dimensional models of the characters they would have to move through imaginary space, sculptors Duke Russell and Charles Cristadoro made little ceramic statues, such as the one of Hyacinth Hippo on point in a tutu, flinging grapes to the hippo chorus line. These statues were even arranged in a miniature mock-up of the set to provide a three-dimensional diagram of the dance.

"In finalizing the characters, a strenuous attempt was made to caricature real bird and animal characteristics rather than to follow cartoon formulas," wrote Ken O'Connor. "To this end, we scaled the precipitous heights of Griffith Park Zoo in search of authenticity. There were no hippos there, which perhaps explains why we had so little trouble drawing them. For all our junketing, it still might be inadvisable to ask whether those are alligators or crocodiles you see on the screen. . . ."

They are alligators, though some of the artists themselves referred to them as "crocs." Crocodiles have narrower snouts, and the fourth tooth on each side of the lower jaw is visible when the mouth is closed. (In alligators, this tooth fits into a socket in the upper jaw.) Besides, the name that the Studio gave the leader of this band of reptilian would-be ravishers should be the tip-off.

He is Ben Ali Gator.

Actually, these animated cartoon characters are interesting and purposeful simplifications of the forms of alligators at the same time that they are interesting and purposeful simplifications of the forms of men. Ben Ali sometimes slithers on his belly like an alligator, more often he walks upright on two feet like a man; he snaps his jaws like an alligator, but he leers and tosses back his red-lined black cape like a lothario on the make.

"In case the complex witchery of other *Fantasia* sequences may lead you to feel that your *Dance of the Hours* has the subtlety of a barn door," wrote Kendall O'Connor, "let me assure you that this is the art that conceals art. In fact, we concealed the art from almost a graphic league of nations. We concealed the art of France in the form of flat pattern à la Matisse, and Picassinine color; and from

Japan, architectural space division and block prints. From Africa we brought masks and weird proportions which we concealed along with the primitive instinct to dance. America and Greece contributed when a rash of dynamic symmetry broke out in the layout room. . . . From Russia, Eisenstein's symphonic principles of handling graphic forms threatened to turn our pencils into batons until this tendency was concealed by crass considerations such as the need for our audience to know what was going on. Into this international morass galloped Unit 2B, with *simplicity* nailed to the masthead and ideals higher than the cost of multiplane."

Unit 2B was the group of animators led by codirector and animation supervisor Norman Ferguson. Simplicity was their goal, and in *Dance of the Hours* they achieved it. Under "Fergy's" supervision, that eclectic range of influences was harnessed to bring three brilliant personalities to life in animation: Mlle. Upanova, the ostrich prima ballerina, with her precarious dignity (and balance); Hyacinth Hippo, the overweight coquette; and Ben Ali Gator, the Valentino lover manqué.

A total of eleven animators did scenes for *Dance of the Hours.* As layout man, O'Connor gave the animators drawings in which were traced in blue pencil the key positions of the characters as they move in the scene, to show the artists the boundaries of the actions they could create.

But now the animators "plussed" (as Walt would say) the plan of action drawn up by the director and layout man by giving the characters the most essential ingredient of an animated film — personality. As codirector of *Dance of the Hours,* Norman Ferguson had consulted with T. Hee and O'Connor during the preparation of the layouts; but now, with the handing out of the scenes to the animators, his most valuable work began — that of animation supervision. Fergy didn't do much of the actual animation. According to Studio records, he was responsible for less than two scenes totaling not quite eleven feet, or about seven seconds of screen time. Such artists as John Lounsbery were better draftsmen than he was. But Fergy's mastery of the staging of broad action is apparent in every scene.

"Fergy was a great help when it came to looking at the pencil tests of the animation," said T. Hee. "Fergy would say to an animator, 'Why don't you exaggerate here? Why don't you pull that leg up a bit?' And he would know how to make a drawing to illustrate the broader action he was after."

To be successful in caricaturing this kind of classical ballet, the Disney animators had to become familiar with the authentic steps and movements that they were to exaggerate. So ballet dancers were brought to the Studio to perform positions and movements for the animators, the equivalent of a model's holding poses for an artist who draws still pictures. Moreover, the Studio shot live-action film of the ballet steps and movements so the animators could have a permanent reference.

"For example," T. Hee said, "we hired a corpulent, wonderful black actress named Hattie Noel, who was not a ballet dancer, to dance like a hippo for us, so that we could study the big flow move-

*Irina Baronova, a dancer with the Ballet Theater, came to the Disney Studio, put on a costume with a few feathers where ostrich feathers would appear, and took the five basic ballet positions. The Character Model Department drew Mlle. Baronova as Mlle. Upanova (above), the ostrich ballerina. At Walt's urging, his story department devised a sequence in which Mlle. Upanova, bearing a cornucopia, throws fruit to the ostrich chorus — with the results seen opposite. The sequence was animated by Howard Swift, Hugh Fraser, and assistant Jerry Hathcock.*

ment of the body. We had a dancer there to show her the steps, and then I would show her certain routines we marked out on the floor of the sound stage and tell her she would have to go there and pirouette here, and then we shot her doing it. She wasn't a dancer, but she was an actress, and she was marvelous.

"And then there was another girl who *was* a ballet dancer. She was a very tall, very ostrichlike girl, and she loved doing the burlesque of the ostrich for us." (Recalled another artist who worked on the sequence, "We put a few feathers on her costume where ostrich feathers should appear, and a bow on her head, and she performed the routine to perfection.")

The *Ostrich Ballet* deals with the five basic ballet positions of the feet as they would be executed by ostriches. Since all of these positions are based upon the exaggerated turn-out of the dancers' feet, there is an opportunity for burlesque inherent in the subject.

"They would seem funny with their big feet," said Walt, and Jack Caldwell pointed out that "their feet look just like ballet slippers. . . . If we open with those [ostriches], we might never know for the first thirty-five bars that they aren't real dancers."

"You never want to get the effect that they're consciously trying to be funny," added Walt. "They're very sincere."

The literal and figurative high point is Mlle. Upanova's pirouette, after which she simply pops up into the air in a dynamic caricature of Nijinsky's famous formula for *jetés*: "You just have to go up there and pause a little." In this scene, animated by Norman Tate, Jerry Hathcock, and Brad Case, she is desperately sincere—and she pauses up there a lot.

In the original storyboards, the sketch artists had Mlle. Upanova throwing flowers to her ostrich *corps de ballet*.

Lee Blair told Walt that "Marge [Belcher, later Champion] did a very nice piece of business there," posing for the live action of the flower-throwing. "She was throwing all over the place."

But Walt wanted it broader, and there follows a striking example of his guiding genius at work: "You know, if we could get it, I would like to see something besides the flower-throwing. That's such an obvious stunt that anybody would do who was burlesquing a ballet. . . . Hey, Jack, you wouldn't want to go out of line there, and she gets a basket of fruit and throws oranges to the ostriches—"

"We had it, and we threw it away," said Lee Blair.

"We thought it was too gaggy," explained Jack Caldwell.

"I tell you, though—is it too gaggy?" asked Walt. "If we took all the stuff, and went overboard too much, then maybe—but just a little touch here and there. It parallels your flower-throwing. It has a certain dignity, and it hasn't—it's your burlesque. There's just time to go overboard and come right back into something legitimate . . . you can't be screwy all the time or it isn't appreciated when you do a good screwy gag."

"Would you want to see the different shapes—bananas and pears—going down their throats?" asked Joe Grant.

Walt would.

*In 1935, Walt Disney put into a memo his thoughts on what animators should be taught. His comments on comedy and caricature help explain why Dance of the Hours is so successful at parodying not only ballet, but various types of human personalities: "Comedy, to be appreciated, must have contact with the audience. . . . By contact, I mean that there must be a familiar, subconscious association. Somewhere, or at some time, the audience has felt, or met with, or seen, or dreamt, the situation pictured. . . . The most hilarious of comedies is always based on things actual, possible, or probable. That idea . . . can be incorporated in every stage of instruction—from the life drawing clear on thru to the planning and staging of the work."*

"One gets a pineapple," said Jim Bodrero, and graphically pantomimed choking.

"The last one could get pineapple—the little clown," said Walt. "I think it's in line just to replace the flower business. Instead of picking the flowers she gets the Horn of Plenty. Then the last thing is like [throwing] the bride's bouquet, or she would go out with the last thing and eat it herself maybe. A whole bunch of grapes she would save. Her whole action is like throwing flowers."

As usual, Disney's instincts were sound. Audience laughter confirms that he had picked the right time, place, and way to "go overboard."

*Hippo Ballet; Afternoon* shows the meaning of caricature being hilariously stretched to contain *moving* caricatures. Walt loved the way that Hyacinth Hippo lampooned centuries of paintings of *The Toilet of Venus.* "This gives you a chance for pantomime and personality," he said, in approving drawings of Hyacinth waking in her pool, powdering, and admiring herself in a mirror. "We can make the audience feel that the hippo thinks she's pretty and tries to look beautiful." (Forty years later, the personality of Miss Piggy would be built on the same basic attitude. "Miss Piggy's not aware of the fact that she's overweight—she dresses as if she's thirty pounds lighter," said Calista Hendrickson, designer of the Muppet star's clothes. "So she has a lot of fantasy.") Hyacinth Hippo wears nothing but a transparent tutu; her abundant fantasy is in full view as she goes into her solo dance.

Fergy started Hyacinth out in her solo dance, then Preston Blair put her through the rest of her paces. And when Blair put the cartoon hippo into a fast spin, he came up with one of the funniest examples of the animation principle of squash and stretch. The principle says that anything composed of living flesh, no matter how bony, will show considerable movement within its shape as it progresses through an action. The shape, in short, will stretch and squash. But this is caricature, the presentation of a person, type, or action distorted to make a point. So as Hyacinth swings around, all her lower anatomy suddenly expands to enormous proportions to make room for the moment when all that weight settles. And when it does settle, her little tail almost disappears in the tightening envelope of flesh.

Walt imagined what he wanted to see here from watching a very slim champion skater and film star named Sonja Henie perform at an ice show. "The way they do these spins," Walt reported at a story conference, is that "Henie spins around and then she sticks that skate in the ice and stops herself, and, gee, when these big fleshy animals do that—it seems to me when they suddenly stop, the damn flesh would come on around and have to come back. That flesh is like a drape—not too vulgar, but to the point where it's funny. You feel that flesh all the time these heavy animals are dancing. It shouldn't be like they're stuffed—you feel it should move around on the bones some, like jelly—it's a jelly effect. When you see a fat woman walk, her arms jiggle and breasts and fanny and everything jiggles. If you watch a fat woman walk, her fanny is just like something hanging loose." Such extreme changes in body shape actually go beyond logic, physical laws, and even, perhaps, the limits of solid draftsmanship;

*Three approaches to the personality of the prima ballerina, Hyacinth Hippo: from a model sheet, a painting of Hyacinth couchant (opposite, above), and a frame from the finished film showing the handmaidens bringing Hyacinth her transparent tutu.*

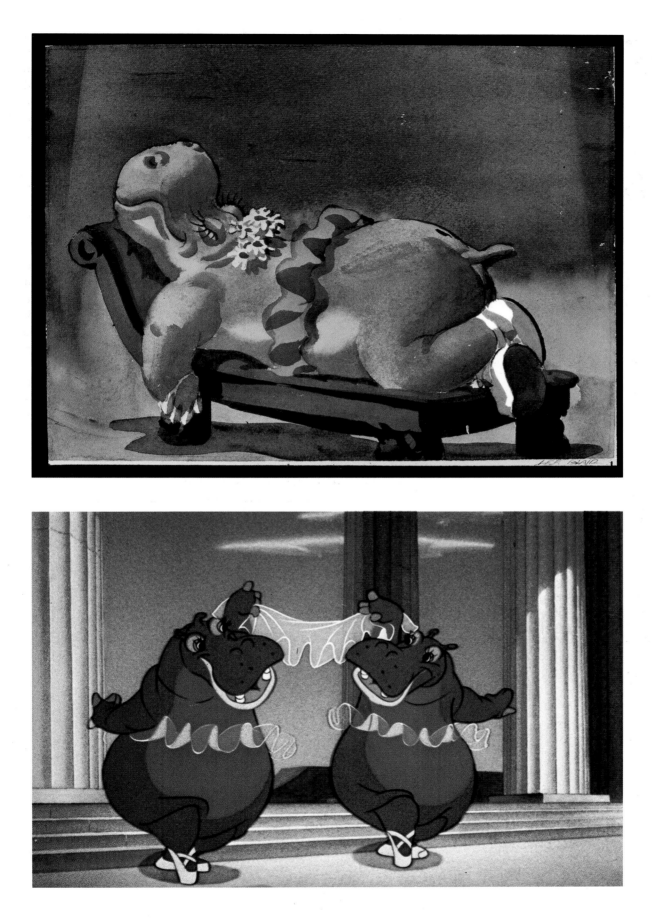

*Give the elephant ballerinas a bubble dance, and dozens of ideas pop out of gag men. In one of them, elephants swish their trunks in a pool and lift them to blow bubbles in the air (opposite, above). Alligators enter the dance, and the bubble blowing, with even more complicated patterns, continues.*

for neither a hippo nor Hattie Noel would ever expand to such a bloated shape. This old style of animation, pioneered by artists like Norman Ferguson, was even then on the way out, making way for a more truly anatomical "life-quality" kind of animation. But in *Dance of the Hours*, it felt right; and when Hyacinth spins up to the camera, stops—and her flesh slowly settles back to normal—one of the great animation caricatures, an overweight belle of the ball in action, has been created.

In *Elephant Ballet; Evening*, a troupe of elephants in ballet costume go to the fountain and blow bubbles, then use them as props in a bubble dance. ("Elephants' trunks can come up and spray like the Beverly Hills fountain," Walt suggested, in a typical example of the way he used everything he saw.)

As a delicious illustration of the segment's low comedy approach to ballet, there is a variation on Charlie Chaplin's old foot-in-the-spittoon gag: Disney's elephants are in line, rolling bubbles down their backs and up in the air. A bubble gets stuck on one elephant's foot, and she tries unsuccessfully to shake it off. Game girl, though—thanks to the animation of Grant Simmons, she keeps dancing with a stiff-legged bounce.

"I still think, on the end, with those elephants, they revert back to—almost to their natural state," Walt had said at an early meeting. "They can't resist grabbing the tail of the one ahead with their trunk and have them run around—you know how an elephant looks when they get them running in a circus. They have a little—I can't do it, but they have a funny little run, the way it keeps going up and down. I think our comedy will come from those natural actions. I like that Heinrich Kley type of stuff.

"What I would like to do is get some of the animators who will work on this stuff in and discuss it—see the possibilities."

In *Alligator Ballet; Night*, the possibilities were superbly realized. "For the crocodiles," said T. Hee, speaking of the alligators,

*In these three illustrations can be seen many of the design ideas of* Dance of the Hours. *Everything in the ostrich sequence was done in verticals and horizontals: the long steps of the ostrich legs, the tall vertical windows through which the blue skies and fleecy clouds of morning can be glimpsed. The camera moved straight up or across at ninety-degree angles. The hippos introduced elliptical movement; their fat forms pirouette around an ellipse of columns and a pool. The camera followed their circular dance, as when Hyacinth spins around the pool. But then Ali Gator runs in (opposite), grabs at Hyacinth, and is caught in the spin. His serpentine is joined to her ellipse. And when Hyacinth and Ben Ali Gator dance their* pas de deux *in the spotlight, the set has changed from day to night, and the dynamic zigzag line of the alligator bodies and actions is carried out in the patterns that the paths make in the gardens.*

"we decided that all the action would be running back and forth across the floor. You would be looking down at the floor and they're running across, chasing a hippo, with their tails flowing out behind them in a zigzag motion." The mad pursuits of romantic ballet are caricatured here by Ben Ali Gator's demented pursuit of the coy ballerina, Hyacinth Hippo.

Johnny Lounsbery became a star animator on *Dance of the Hours.* Not surprisingly, Ben Ali Gator remained his favorite character to the end of his life. John had been Fergy's assistant on the Wicked Witch in *Snow White,* and he had done some fine scenes with the crafty fox and stupid cat in Fergy's unit on *Pinocchio,* but when he set the character of Ben Ali Gator in motion, it made his reputation. In 1971 Lounsbery reminisced about the way that he and layout man Kendall O'Connor gave Walt what he had seen vaguely in his imagination many months before: a crocodile appearing "up on a high thing," giving out with a " 'Hah!' sort of hissing," and leaping out on the floor.

"Ken laid out that opening shot on the croc—a pretty effective thing where you have an upshot of the pillar, and as the croc curled down the pillar, you went from an upshot to a downshot—a real long vertical pan that created a beautiful effect."

But it wasn't only in space that Lounsbery's animation succeeded; he was a master of timing. "It was the first time I had worked with music to that extent," he recalled, "where you are completely guided by the tempo and accents of a prescored sound track. Our readings of the track covered three, four—sometimes five—columns, as they read all these instruments—and it was a lot of fun trying to be inventive enough to fit action to all these sounds."

The reading of the sound track recorded on Lounsbery's exposure sheet showed him exactly where each instrument picked up and left off and where the accents were in the music. "The best example was on the croc," said Lounsbery. "He'd slide down the pillar and hit a pose on the accent in the music."

Many animators feel that an even better example of Lounsbery's brilliant animation was the way that Ben Ali walked. Since all the alligators were designed to look alike and be dressed alike, Lounsbery made Ben Ali stand out from the others by giving him a bright, cocky walk that showed he was boss.

The topper in this constantly building comedy of gags was contributed by T. Hee, then animated by Lounsbery, just before the drawings were cleaned up to be inked and painted. Hyacinth stands on one leg with her other leg raised behind her in a perfect arabesque. Ben Ali walks around her, pivoting her on her toe, in a *pirouette en arabesque.* He stops and pushes her into a spin, like a boy on a playground pushing a girl on a merry-go-round. He repeats the spin. Then he gets an idea—and hops a ride on her outstretched leg.

"As a picture moved along, from the story conferences to the director to the layout man to the animators, Walt never stopped polishing it, plussing it, improving it," Dick Huemer explained. "That was the beauty of Walt's place. It was never finished until it was previewed. And even then it wasn't finished sometimes."

*A harpy shrieks up to the camera on Walpurgis Night, hair red, eyes purple, lips green, visage demonic.*

# MOUNTAIN/AVE MARIA

The last number in *Fantasia* is a combination of two pieces of music utterly different in construction and mood, whose synergism was intended as a dramatic example of the struggle between the profane and the sacred. The first is *Night on Bald Mountain,* a tone poem by Modest Moussorgsky. The second is *Ave Maria,* by Franz Schubert. In this arrangement, the end of the first piece blends without pause into the second, so that the bells heralding the morning in *Night on Bald Mountain* seem to be the bells calling the faithful to worship in the *Ave Maria.*

Moussorgsky first sketched *Night on Bald Mountain* in 1860 for solo piano and orchestra, then rewrote it in 1868, 1871, and 1875. It was never performed during the composer's lifetime. In 1882, Moussorgsky's friend Rimsky-Korsakov revised and reorchestrated the work and conducted that version at its first performance in 1886. It was the Rimsky-Korsakov arrangement that Leopold Stokowski recorded for *Fantasia* in 1939, but when Irwin Kostal conducted the digital rerecording of the *Fantasia* sound track in 1982, he used Moussorgsky's own, more savage orchestration.

The German lyrics for Schubert's song were translated from Sir Walter Scott's *The Lady of the Lake.* The English text was written especially for *Fantasia* by Rachel Field.

Bald Mountain is Mount Triglaf, an eminence near Kiev in southern Russia. Here, according to Slavonic mythology, evil spirits gather on Walpurgis Night, the equivalent of our Halloween, to worship the devil.

The pattern of the music and the animated pictures is the pattern of the Witches' Sabbath itself. First, Chernobog, the god of evil and death, appears out of the top of Bald Mountain. He gathers to him the evil ones—witches, demons, vampires, and the skeletons of corpses not buried in consecrated ground. They dance furiously as his Satanic majesty condemns them, by giant handfuls, to the fiery pit inside the mountain. It is his perverse pleasure to transform some of these demons into animals before throwing them into the flames, and he is reaching for more evil ones to play with when the bells heralding the morning drive the ghosts back to their graveyard, the evil spirits back to the town, and the cringing Chernobog back into Bald Mountain.

These same morning bells that make the devil fold his wings around himself and again become a mountaintop call the faithful to the worship of the God of Love. A procession of figures carrying lights is seen faintly through the drifting morning fog at the base of the mountain. The procession crosses a bridge, their lights reflected in the water below. As the solemn file ascends a hill, gothic tree forms emerge from the fog, suggesting the sanctuary of a church. The procession passes along the edge of a quiet pool. In the distance, we see a pulsating light that gradually assumes a form suggesting a cathedral window. The camera glides through the window, comes out into a predawn sky, and a sunburst fills the sky with color as the choir sings the last chords of the *Ave Maria.*

"To captivate our varied and worldwide audience of all ages," said Walt Disney, "the nature and treatment of the fairy tale, the legend, the myth, have to be elementally simple. Good and evil, the antagonists of all great drama in some guise, must be believably personalized. The moral ideas common to all humanity must be upheld."

The conflict between good and evil had been Disney's primary theme since Mickey Mouse first confronted Peg-Leg Pete. The contrast of Moussorgsky's violent *Night on Bald Mountain* with Schubert's tranquil *Ave Maria* as the conclusion of *Fantasia* was his most ambitious statement of that theme. The defect of this conclusion is that the evil was expressed so much more effectively than the good, a frequent problem in all forms of art. The great strength of this segment is that its personification of evil in Vladimir Tytla's animation of Chernobog, the Black God or Satan, was and remains today the highest point yet achieved in the art of animation.

All of Disney's best work is an allegorical representation of the triumph of life and hope over the powers of despair and death. Death is personified as the Wicked Witch in *Snow White and the Seven Dwarfs,* the hunters in *Bambi,* Tetti Tatti, the impresario who did not believe in miracles, in *The Whale Who Wanted to Sing at the Met,* Cruella DeVil, the villainess of *One Hundred and One Dalmatians,* and Maleficent, the wicked enchantress of *Sleeping Beauty.* Despair is depicted in the scenes with Monstro the whale in *Pinocchio,* the mad elephant cage for Dumbo's mother, the destructive stepmother in *Cinderella,* and the grotesque and menacing Tulgey Wood in which Alice gets lost in Wonderland. But none of these representations had the mythic force of Chernobog, who is the god of evil in Slavonic mythology.

"At the basis of Slavonic mythology we find a primitive dualism which had its source in the opposition between light, the creative force, and darkness, the destructive force," the new *Larousse Encyclopedia of Mythology* tells us. "This elemental opposition gave birth to two divine images which are found among the peoples of the Western branch of the Slavonic world: Byelobog and Chernobog. The composition of their names reveals their characters. Byelobog is made up of the adjective 'byely,' which means 'white,' and the noun 'bog,' which means 'god.' The adjective 'cherny' on the other hand means 'black.' Thus there is a white god, god of light and day, and a black god, god of the shadows and of night: a god of good and a god of evil, opposed one to the other. . . . The Ukrainians still say, 'May the black god exterminate you.' "

This dualism fit perfectly Disney's dictum that "the nature and treatment of . . . the myth, have to be elementally simple." However, as a Christian artist, he chose to place in opposition to the god of evil not Byelobog, the pagan god of good, pictured in Slavonic mythology as an old man with a white beard, dressed in white, but instead a procession of worshippers seeking the intercession of the Blessed Virgin Mary, mother of the Christian God.

To supervise the animation of this segment and personally to animate the god of evil, Walt Disney chose Vladimir Tytla, who had previously animated the Seven Dwarfs, most memorably Grumpy, in *Snow White,* the passionate Stromboli in *Pinocchio,* and the menacing giant in *The Brave Little Tailor.*

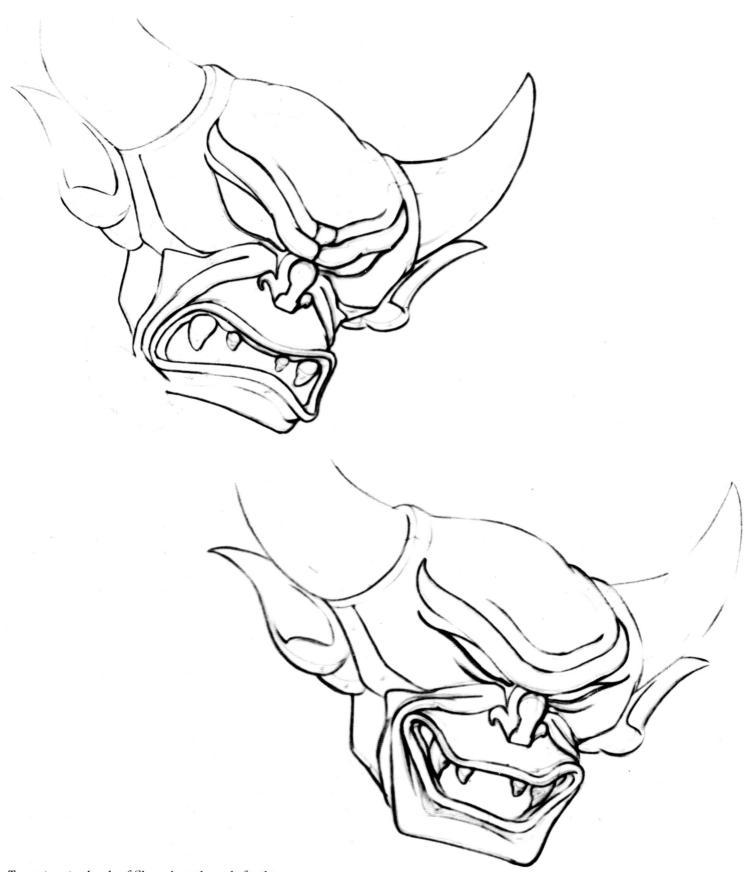

*Two grimacing heads of Chernobog, the god of evil in Slavonic mythology: a frown and a malignant smile.*

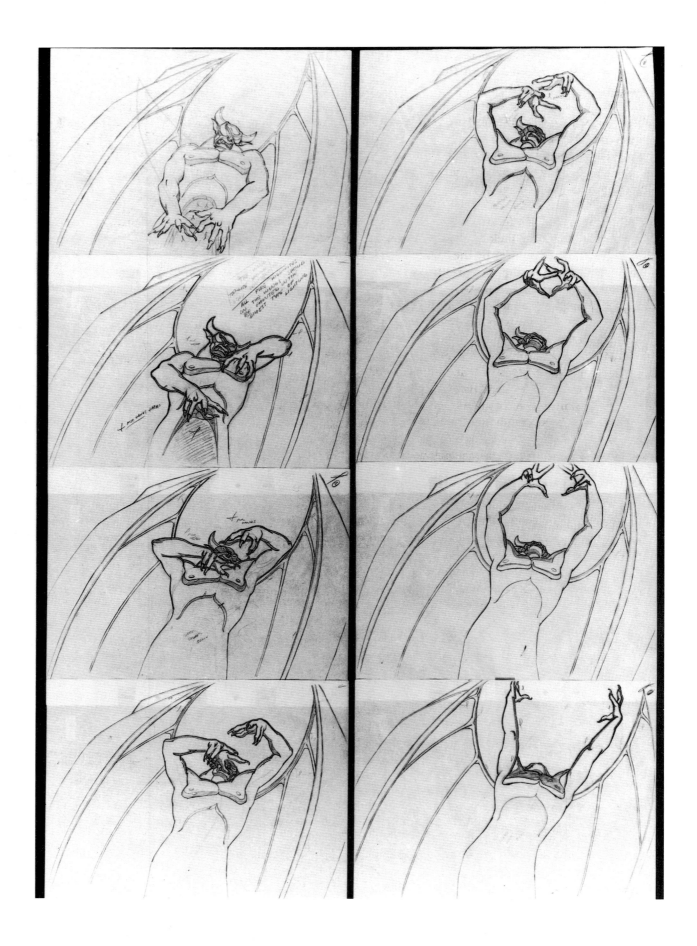

"I'm Ukrainian," said Tytla, a gentle New Yorker whose black mustache made him look like a fierce Cossack. "My father was a Ukrainian cavalryman. On all my animation I tried to do some research and look into the background of each character. I studied Italians for weeks to do Stromboli. But I could relate immediately to this character. Ukrainian folklore is based on Chernobog. Moussorgsky used terms I could understand."

The Disney version of *Night on Bald Mountain* follows closely the program appended to the original printed score of Moussorgsky's tone poem: "A subterranean din of unearthly voices. Appearance of the Spirits of Darkness, followed by that of Chernobog. Glorification of the Black God. The Black Mass. The Revelry of the Witches' Sabbath, interrupted from afar by the bell of a little church, whereupon the spirits of evil disperse. Dawn breaks."

The Disney visualization of Chernobog, however, sprang from an inspirational pencil sketch by Albert Hurter. Hurter, a middle-aged Swiss bachelor who had been an animator on *Mutt and Jeff* in the twenties, never animated for Disney. But he had a fantastic visual imagination, expressed entirely in pencil sketches, so Disney paid him to sit by himself all day and fill sheet after sheet with drawings that would inspire Disney's other artists. "The demon on top of Bald Mountain was his idea," said story director Dick Huemer. "A simple pencil sketch showing the demon up there unfolding his wings suggested the whole thing to us."

To design his Witches' Sabbath, however, Walt Disney went outside his Studio for talent and hired Kay Nielsen, one of the finest contemporary illustrators of myths and fairy tales. *East of the Sun, West of the Moon* was probably his best-known work.

Wilfred Jackson, who had directed one of the greatest Disney cartoon shorts, *The Band Concert*, directed the segment. Jackson shot live action of Bela Lugosi, the screen's famous Dracula, for Tytla to study for the movements of the devil. But the way that Lugosi unfolded his "wings" and gestured was not the way that Tytla saw those movements in his imagination. So after Lugosi left, Tytla had the skinny Jackson bare his chest and move the way that Tytla directed him to move for the motion picture camera. "I even did the hocus pocus thing with the little guys on my hands," said Jackson, alluding to Chernobog's fistfuls of flames that changed into demons and beasts.

Looking at this live action, at three-dimensional models of Chernobog that the Character Model Department had sculpted, and deep into his imagination, Bill Tytla animated the devil.

"It was one of the greatest things I've ever seen in my life," said Marc Davis, himself one of the finest draftsman/animators in the history of the art. "I think that was the high point. The whole thing comes to life. The moment of fear when the bell begins to toll stands out, but I like the shape of this whole thing. It was enormous.

"But, you see, this could only happen at the Disney Studio — because it wasn't only Bill. You had Kay Nielsen, who sketched this thing up. And it was pretty much as it was on the screen. You had sculptors who made models. And you had Bill Tytla, who was just

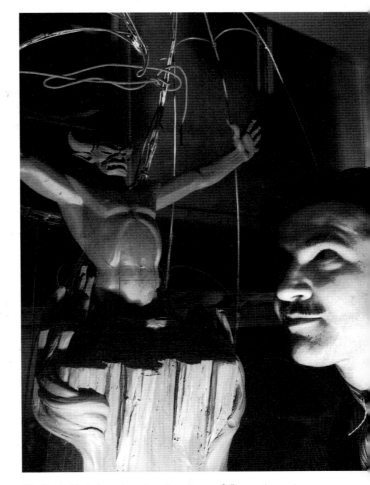

*Vladimir Tytla's animation drawings of Chernobog, the devil on Bald Mountain, make a powerful gesture out of the act of raising his hands (opposite). Tytla examines the model of Chernobog with outstretched arms that was sculpted at the Studio to enable the master animator to see the character in three dimensions. The devil was even shown coming out of a model mountaintop with wings made as wire sculptures. As a young man, Tytla had studied sculpture in Paris, and throughout his life his drawings had a sculptural quality.*

185

DEVIL MODEL
BARE MOUNTAIN
2004 SEQ 11.0

THIS MATERIAL IS THE PROPERTY OF WALT DISNEY PRODUCTIONS IT IS UNPUBLISHED AND MUST NOT BE TAKEN FROM THE STUDIO DUPLICATED OR USED IN ANY MANNER EXCEPTING FOR PRODUCTION PURPOSES WITHOUT WRITTEN PERMISSION FROM AN AUTHORIZED OFFICER OF THE COMPANY.

*Danish-born illustrator Kay Nielsen created this devil model for* Night on Bald Mountain. *The two pastels (opposite) were explorations—not used—of how the devil might crush his worshipers and how he might reach down to scoop them out of the crater. This scene was memorably animated by Bill Tytla.*

right at that moment to do something like this. He had all the art in the world in him at that moment. He died a thousand deaths after he left the Studio. He never really belonged in any other place. So I like to remember Bill doing this picture — the right time and the right place for everything he had to offer."

Personal responsibilities made it necessary for Tytla to leave the Disney Studio and return to the East in 1943, and until he died, on December 29, 1969, at the age of sixty-four, he worked in New York, first for Paramount, where he directed *Popeye, Little Lulu,* and *Little Audrey* cartoons, and later producing television commercials. When this writer urged him to attend the First World Retrospective of Animation Cinema, held in conjunction with the 1967 World's Fair in Montreal, Tytla asked: "Do you think they'll know who I am?"

He was astonished to receive an ovation at Expo '67 from colleagues, critics, and filmgoers from all over the world. He was the first animator, as Frank Thomas and Ollie Johnston later acknowledged, to achieve strong emotions and convincing acting with the human figure, but he didn't know that so many people were aware of what he had accomplished, or that so many viewed *Bald Mountain* as the peak of Disney's achievement.

Yet Disney had been worried, when he began story conferences on the Moussorgsky composition, that he was overreaching himself. "What I'm thinking about is this," he said. "We have done cartoon and comic bats and cats, and we have used graves and spooks from graves. It's quite obvious; there is nothing new about it. In this thing we are attempting to do something bigger than we are able to handle, to tell the truth. We want to go beyond those obvious things we have done. We're getting all mixed up here and nothing is coming out of it. It's just an attempt to do something big, but it's falling flat. We have to have more than just a bunch of pictures on the screen."

Disney first treated the theme of a Walpurgis Night (or Witches' Sabbath, or Halloween), when the spirits of the dead come out of their graves at midnight and revel until dawn, in 1929 in his first Silly Symphony, *The Skeleton Dance.* But that first attempt was strictly comic, with no suggestion that the skeletons were the spirits of those not buried in consecrated ground, and with "cartoon and comic bats and cats" that were not very convincing as symbols of evil.

"Oh, hell! They have always used cats to symbolize evil," snapped Walt at one story conference, rejecting black cats as a story element in *Night on Bald Mountain.*

Instead, to the demonic music of Moussorgsky, the Disney Studio animated nothing less than "Satan and the other evil spirits who roam through the world seeking the ruin of souls." Because of Kay Nielsen, these demons were strikingly well designed; because of Terrell Stapp and Charles Payzant, their careers through the sulfurous air were eerily choreographed; because of the animation supervision of Tytla and the actual animation of Tytla, William N. Shull, Don Patterson, and others, they moved with the horrid realism of creatures in a nightmare: witches riding goats, witches riding wild boars, the ghosts of warriors riding the skeletons of horses and cows, "the souls, and often the skeletons, of those not buried in consecrated

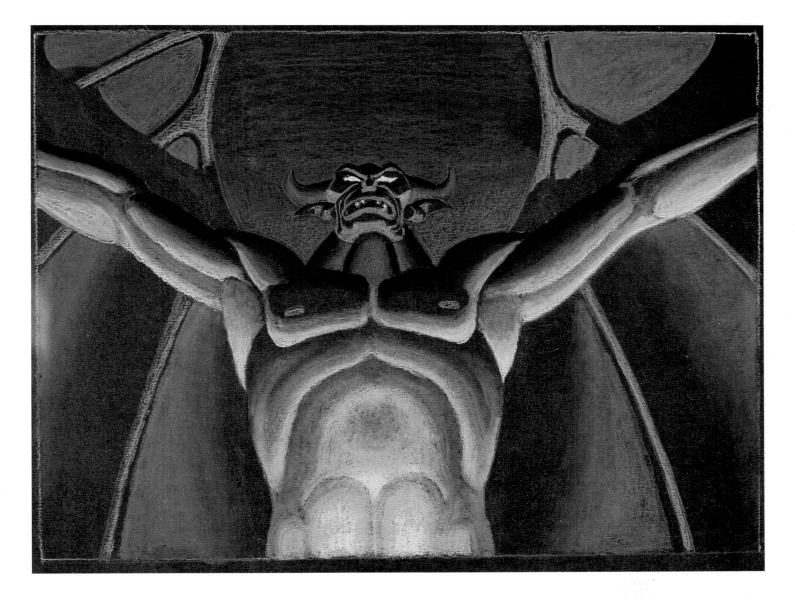

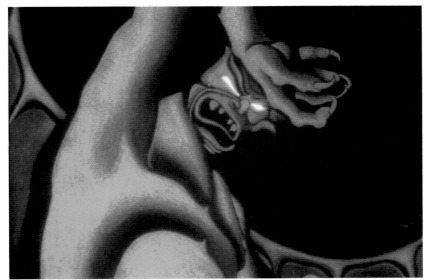

Kay Nielsen's storyboard sketches (opposite) illustrate
the moment when Chernobog unfolds his wings and
begins to cast a spell on the village at the foot of Bald
Mountain. Nielsen renders a triumphant Chernobog
(above) and a cringing Chernobog with his hand
covering his forehead, trying to protect himself from
the sound of Christian church bells. Nielsen created a
visually dynamic pattern that responded to the auditory
pattern in the music, and the animators created
a world in which the image and the sound are fused.

A model sheet is specific about the shapes and forms of the evil spirits who sweep around the base of Bald Mountain, lured upward by the devil's beckoning hands. Kay Nielsen's original storyboard sketches (opposite) of the evil spirits were less detailed, but contain the essence of the forms.

ground; also such living humans as have sold their souls to the devil," as one old book describes the damned.

Special animation effects and special camera effects add further to the expressiveness of this invocation of damnation and evil. Such an elementary device as ripple glass makes wispy ghosts seem to writhe in the wind as they rise from their graves trailing rotting shrouds and tattered winding sheets. Other effects are the result of sophisticated and painstaking labor. Daniel MacManus was given some scenes in which flames dancing on Chernobog's hand would metamorphose into the shapes of the damned.

"They should give the impression of being female forms," he was told. "But if they look like women, they're no good. And if they don't look like women, they're no good."

Such plausibly impossible assignments were what animation was for. MacManus animated fire that appears to be taking the shapes of three women, then changes into the shapes of a wolf, a pig, and a goat. These three animals change into six demons. The devil turns his hand over, then back, and the demons scramble around to keep on the top side of the hand. Chernobog closes his hand on them, anyway, crushing the demons. When he opens his hand again, they have turned to six flames.

This special effects animation fits with Tytla's powerful drawing and animation of Chernobog's hands—the hands for which Wilfred Jackson's were the models. A moment later, when the devil lowers his hands into the flames inside Bald Mountain, the flames burst up in four accented movements, synchronized with four big accents in the music. As the demons dance on the crater's edge, the colors change on the music phrase. Director Wilfred Jackson had come a long way from the days when he played his harmonica for *Steamboat Willie* while Ub Iwerks fitted his animation of Mickey Mouse to the accents in the music.

The next moment of *Fantasia* brought sound and sight together in a way never before possible. The sound, as Leopold Stokowski afterward described it, is "an extremely powerful chord . . . played by all the horns, trumpets, trombones, tuba—with deep foundation tones by tympani, bass drum, and tamtam. Above this chord all the string and woodwind instruments play a rapid rushing-down passage, beginning very high and ending with the lowest tones of the double basses. These downward-rushing tones should sound like an avalanche—beginning loud and increasing in tonal volume the lower they go. In the concert hall this is impossible to achieve because the instruments have more strength of tone in their higher registers than in their lower, so that no matter how much the players try to increase the volume as the tones become deeper, exactly the opposite happens—the volume of the tone becomes less. In *Fantasia* we were able for the first time to achieve the ideal in this music—increasing the tone as the scale passage descended—because recording for motion pictures puts techniques at our disposal whereby the 'impossible' can sometimes be achieved. When these techniques are further developed the whole idea of 'impossible' will be forever set aside—because everything will be possible in the tonal sphere."

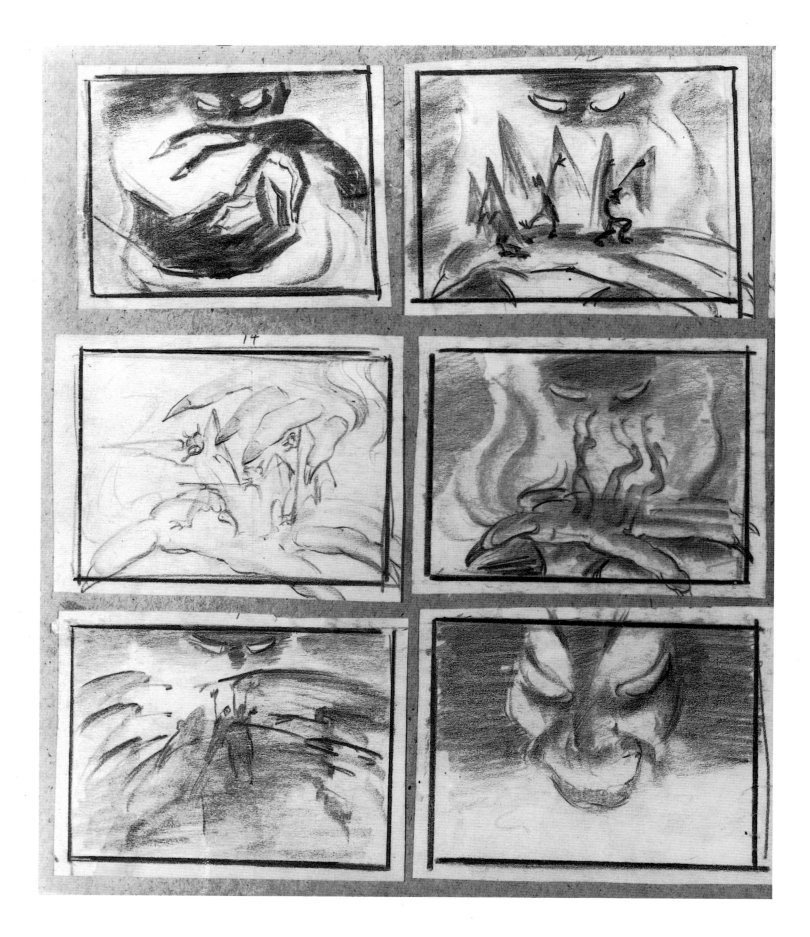

The visualization of evil spirits in storyboard sketches (opposite) and suggested color models (above) resulted in the final animation on the screen, including Bill Shull's memorable ghost riding a skeleton cow.

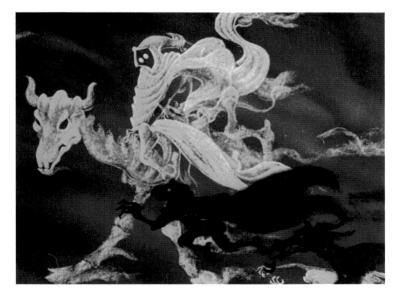

The sight—the complement to this passage in the visual sphere—is the climactic moment of Satan's revel. Chernobog has been casting fiends into the flames, and we have been looking down with him into the bottomless pit. Now, suddenly, we are looking up at this mountainous Prince of Darkness, as he transforms all these evil spirits into one shooting yellow flame, which he thrusts like a lightning bolt into hell, whence it lights up his loins.

In the interval of silence following this avalanche of sound, the devil reaches into the pit to scoop the accursed up again, and he is stretching down when the tolling of a bell disturbs him. He glances up—where is the hateful sound coming from? Ah, no matter—go at them again. But the bell tolls a second time, and he raises one arm, as if to ward off a blow. The bell tolls a third time, and the devil cowers, as if the sound were of a frequency to break his eardrums. He puts his hand over his eyes. He lowers his other hand in the agony that devils are said to feel at the sound of a bell. Defeated, the devil folds his wings and becomes again the peak of Bald Mountain.

"In spite of the helplessness and horror inspired by the dark forces which lurk in and behind our world and have power to estrange it," wrote Wolfgang Kayser in *The Grotesque in Art and Literature*, "the truly artistic portrayal effects a secret liberation. The darkness has been sighted, the ominous powers discovered, the incomprehensible forces challenged. And thus we arrive at a final interpretation of the grotesque: An attempt to invoke and subdue the demonic aspects of the world."

When Bill Tytla was asked by this writer how he approached the animation of the devil on Bald Mountain, he drew himself up, like an actor getting back into an old role. "I imagined that I was as big as a mountain and made of rock and yet I was feeling and moving," Tytla answered. Then he dropped the devil's posture and became a man again. "You see?"

He had demonstrated his Chernobog. But it was still a mystery how he had managed to convey the feelings he imagined through a series of drawings projected on a screen at the rate of twenty-four frames a second. That is the mystery of animation.

Tytla shared with Disney an overwhelming empathy, a fellow-feeling with all creation that was almost Franciscan. "You know," he once said, "we approached those things with a great deal of emotion." He could identify with Doc, Dopey, Sleepy, Sneezy, Happy, Bashful, and Grumpy; with Stromboli, Pinocchio's puppet master; the giant conquered by Mickey in *The Brave Little Tailor*; little Dumbo; and the devil himself . . . and make us feel their emotions.

What Stokowski said of Disney, the producer of animation, was true also of Tytla, his greatest animator: "His imagination, humor, insight, sense of design and ability to enter into the life of feeling of any man or animal, tree or stone, and make us feel with him, are the delight of millions of children, and grown-up children, all over the world."

194

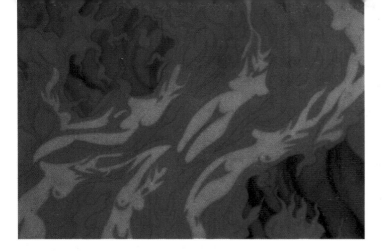

"The darkness has been sighted, and ominous powers discovered, the incomprehensible forces challenged," wrote Wolfgang Kayser in The Grotesque in Art and Literature. He defined the grotesque as "an attempt to invoke and subdue the demonic aspects of the world." The picturization of the demonic in Night on Bald Mountain ranged from Kay Nielsen's inspirational sketches to the finished frames.

195

Nielsen came to Los Angeles in 1936, working as an actor, director, set designer, and muralist until his death in 1957. Out of that period came his designs for Night on Bald Mountain and Ave Maria.

# AVE MARIA

**O**ne day in December, 1938, while working on the *Ave Maria* section of *Fantasia,* Walt Disney got "a little riled up," and said as much about his hopes for his medium as he ever did. He and his story staff had just listened to a record of Schubert's song, and they had looked at the sketches on the storyboards showing pilgrims going to church in the early morning, carrying candles. Now, one of the storymen said, "I always wonder if we're taking full advantage of the cartoon medium, with a picture like this."

"This is not 'the cartoon medium,' " Walt snapped. "It should not be limited to cartoons. We have worlds to conquer here."

This was Walt Disney the risk-taking adventurer speaking. Among Disney's competitors that year, Max Fleischer received an Academy Award nomination for a cartoon called *Hunky and Spunky,* but Disney got the other four nominations and won the Oscar for his animation of the Munro Leaf–Robert Lawson juvenile bestseller *Ferdinand the Bull.* M-G-M was animating the old comic strip *Captain and the Kids*; the stars of Warner Brothers cartoons were Porky Pig and Daffy Duck; Walter Lantz was still making cartoons with Disney's 1927 character creation, Oswald the Rabbit; and Paul Terry, who dominated film animation when Disney came to Hollywood in 1923, finally produced a cartoon in color, six years after Disney did, a version of Jack and the Beanstalk called *String Bean Jack.*

This was the professional atmosphere in which Disney was planning the *Ave Maria* as, explained the *Fantasia* program, "an emotional relief to audiences tense from the shock of Moussorgsky's malignant music and its grim visualization.

"In a universal language, music, the *Ave Maria* sings of peace and hope and life," Disney's program continued. "Schubert himself said it was written as an act of spontaneous devotion springing from an overpowering emotion.

"Crossing the natural bridge of music from *Bald Mountain* to *Ave Maria,* far away in the dim light of first dawn is seen a band of hooded pilgrims carrying torches. They move through avenues of tall-trunked trees. As the light increases, the trees take on natural gothic forms until the forest seems to have become the interior of a cathedral, immense, stately and beautiful beyond the dreams of human architects."

To the objection that such a conception did not take full advantage of the animation medium, Walt replied: "The best answer I can think of is this: that we've got an hour and forty-five minutes of picture, and we're doing beautiful things with beautiful music. We're doing comic things, fantastic things, and it can't all be the same. It's an experimental thing, and I'm willing to experiment on it. We've got more in this medium than making people laugh. We love to make people laugh, but I think we can do both.

"This covers four minutes in our picture, and it's going to be four precious minutes when we're through—the beauty we can get from controlled color and the music and everything we use here will be worth it. This stuff means more, it's richer, it's like a painting. . . . People go all over Europe to look at cathedrals, and when you go in they don't look like this—you don't see the beauty there.

You have to get back and squint your eyes, or you have to see it at a certain hour or a certain minute of the day."

"This will give you all those minutes together," said Dick Huemer, getting into the spirit of the thing.

"It's only four minutes," Walt continued. "I'm looking at this and *Clair de lune* as a chance to — as a contrast to what we have before and after it." (*Clair de lune* was later cut from *Fantasia*, though the visual complement created was included in *Make Mine Music* in 1946 with a popular choral ballad called *Blue Bayou*.) "I don't want us to get too much animation in this — it doesn't need it, and animators are scarce. It gives us a chance to get the stuff out, and look what it gives the background a chance to do."

And in fact, the *Ave Maria* was planned as the greatest showcase ever provided for the background painter's talents and skills, supported by dramatic camera angles from the layout man and special photographic images from the effects animators and the optical wizards in the camera department.

The sequence begins with a spectacular cross dissolve. Tytla had animated the devil in medium close-up, folding his wings around himself and metamorphosing once more into the top of Bald Mountain. Now the camera trucks back until the screen is filled with drifting fog. The shot was designed for the Academy Award-winning multiplane camera, which gives the illusion of depth to the flat character drawings and background paintings of two-dimensional animation. Of the more than eleven thousand two hundred feet of film shot for *Fantasia*, thirty-five hundred feet were multiplane footage, more than in *Snow White* and *Pinocchio* combined. The capability of the camera is best shown in scenes like this, where it seems to envelop Bald Mountain and its valley in three-dimensional space.

These scenes "called for quite a bit of processing, meaning, of course, the double and triple printing and the process dissolves from one scene to another, and also dissolves within the scenes themselves," wrote Ed Gershman (later a founding member of UPA, the studio that produced *Mr. Magoo* and *Gerald McBoing-Boing*). Gershman worked on the innovative *Ave Maria* and found that "much of this was mostly experimental, not only for the [Disney] Studio, but also for Technicolor."

Lights move into the scene from camera left and across the scene to camera right, alternately obscured and revealed by the drifting fog. The procession crosses a bridge — but the figures are still obscured by fog. Fog and mist are particularly difficult to animate: you can't put a pencil line around them. But greater animation challenges are to come.

The lights reflect in the water below the bridge, the halation forming a cross in the reflection. The ripples in the water break up the reflection.

Now, in a vast panorama stretching across 118 feet of film (each foot of film contains sixteen frames), the figures in the procession become visible through the fog. Gothic tree forms emerge from the fog as the procession climbs the hill. The lights suggest the stained-glass windows and the tree forms resemble the arched sanc-

*The struggle between the profane and the sacred, which was what Walt Disney wanted to symbolize with his juxtaposition of* Night on Bald Mountain *and* Ave Maria, *had long been the primary subject of the art of Kay Nielsen. In these frames from the film we see the strength of evil represented by Chernobog, and the strength of good symbolized by the reflection of light in water as the figures climb a hill past the delicate tracery of typical Nielsen trees.*

This caricature of Walt Disney (above) was reproduced in the original Fantasia program with the following note: "The obviously anonymous artist who drew this sketch of the Boss titled it 'I don't like it!' Walt Disney's facial expression is one that his staff frequently sees when he confronts something that is good, but not good enough." When Walt raised that eloquent eyebrow . . .

Artists at the Disney Studio were excited by this large inspirational watercolor, with its high streaming light effects and nuns bearing candles, created by Kay Nielsen for Ave Maria (opposite). Master animators Frank Thomas and Ollie Johnston have written of Nielsen's design that "the glow of the candles carried by the hooded figures proved to be an impossible problem in production, but the glory of this concept for the scene made everyone keep trying."

tuary of a church. Still in long shot, the pilgrims pass along the edge of a quiet pool. The camera trucks down to the reflections in the water, then moves ahead of the reflections, so the scene ends on a dark, quiet part of the water.

"Some of the closest animation ever attempted by any animator in the Studio was the animation of the nuns in the long pan," wrote Gershman. In animation, the slower the movement, the more drawings there are, and the closer together each successive drawing of the same figure is. "So close was this animation," Gershman wrote, "that the difference in the width of a pencil line was more than enough to cause 'jitters,' not only to the animation, but to everyone connected with the sequence." (Jitters, also called "strobing," occur when the successive images of a progressive movement are not fused by the persistence of vision, but appear to move as a series of short, staccato jumps—in short, to jitter.)

Again and again, Walt was dissatisfied with the way the Ave Maria looked, and he ordered expensive and time-consuming retakes. The optimism and self-confidence with which he had begun Fantasia was being assaulted by the hard facts of a world at war. The European market that was his profit margin was cut off from the expensive Pinocchio and would be cut off from all his pictures until the war ended. By the summer of 1940, it was clear that Pinocchio, which had been released in February, would not recover its $2.6 million cost. And the difficult Bambi would not be finished until sometime in 1942. Now, much more was riding on the experimental Fantasia than Disney had intended. And yet his reaction to these dire circumstances was not to get it out, but to get it perfect. Ultimately, all decisions at the Walt Disney Studio were made, or were subject to review, by Walt Disney, as this memo to his coworkers from Wilfred Jackson, director of Night on Bald Mountain and Ave Maria, clearly shows: "In a conversation with Walt today, it develops that he is doubtful as to whether we should have a Madonna in Ave Maria at all . . ." wrote Jackson, referring to Walt's original plan to show a Madonna in the sky at the end of the film. "If possible, it would be best to shoot the Madonna separately from the sky, so she may be double-printed in or left out at will, after the shooting is done. In case this is not practical, we must either get a decision from Walt, as to whether she is in or out before the scene is shot, or else shoot this part of the scene two ways, once with the Madonna and clouds, and once with only the clouds. Gail Papineau will be responsible for contacting Walt on this matter before the scene is shot.

"If the sky with the underlighting on the clouds and the sunburst is designed while I am away, Ray Lockrem will check directly with Walt, and get Walt's approval of the design and setup before the scene is shot.

"Walt wants to be sure we have a good finish for this sequence and for the Concert Feature, and that this sunburst sky will be a decorative and colorful one."

On August 2, 1940, six artists and a secretary sat with Walt while the Ave Maria reel was run.

"Where do we get all that jitter in there?" asked Walt.

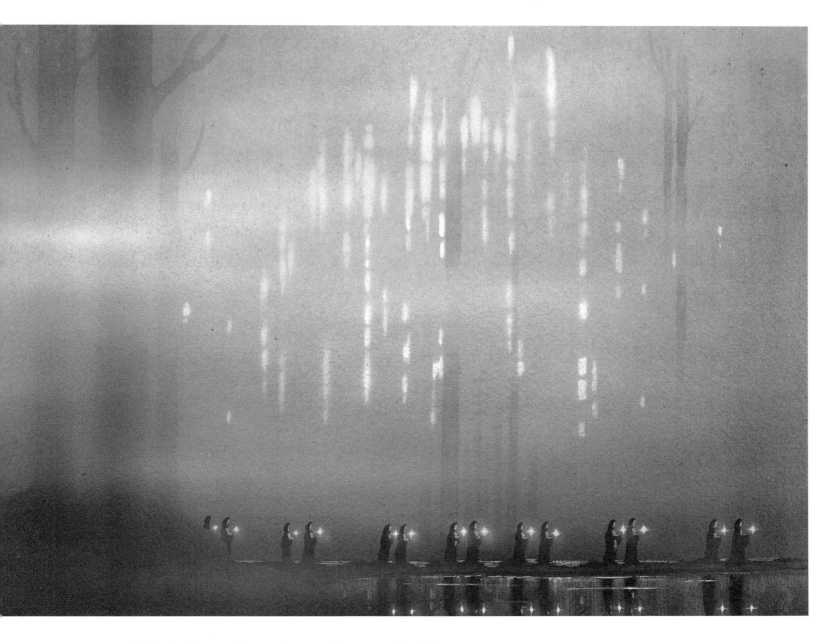

"It looks like it is from inking and painting," said Papineau.

"It's a lousy job," said Walt. "We can't use it. Both the lights and the figures jitter. We can't have it in this thing. It looks like the speed of the characters is a little fast, too."

For the rest of the meeting of an hour and a half, the seven artists discussed how to fix the problem. The solutions would take time and be expensive, but Walt was set on getting on the screen what he had seen in his mind the previous January, when he rejected some story sketches, saying, "Pretty scenes aren't going to carry this. It must be like a spectacle on the stage. It can't be too literal in its interpretation. It must glorify the sacred side as 'Bare Mountain' does the profane side. It is too subtle, this way. There must be a bigness to it, to fit the way we expect to present this music."

The last scene in the *Ave Maria* visualization is probably the

Kay Nielsen's inspirational sketches for Ave Maria, such as the one at right, had the figures in the procession becoming visible through fog, gothic tree forms emerging from fog as the procession climbs the hill, and the light from the candles reflected in a quiet pool. John McManus created the light and fog effects seen in the frames above and on the opposite page.

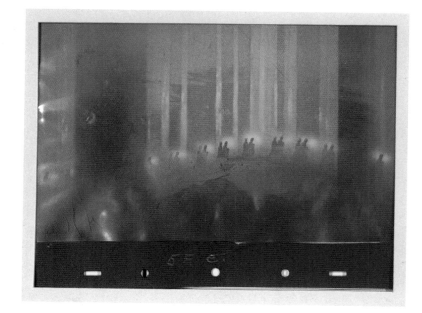

longest scene in an animated film up to that time—217 feet! It is a long shot that begins on a velvety black surface with a pulsating light shining in deep space. The camera trucks toward the light, through those tree forms suggesting the interior of a cathedral, through the "window," and out into the predawn sky. The sunburst fills the sky with color as the scene—and the film—fade out.

In an early story conference that dealt with combining *Night on Bald Mountain* with *Ave Maria*, Walt Disney said, "The forces of good on one side and of evil on the other is what I'm trying to see in this thing." Deems Taylor described the procession in the *Ave Maria* as "a vast host of worshippers" of the God of Light, in contradistinction to the worshippers of the Prince of Darkness on Bald Mountain. "On moves the procession, on and on," he wrote, "until we reach the end and emerge in a blaze of morning light. Once again the powers of life and hope have triumphed over the hosts of death and despair."

The story of how that last shot was put on film says the final word on the spirit of adventure with which Disney and his staff approached *Fantasia.* When Disney told his special effects artists what he wanted for *Fantasia*'s last scene, there were only a few weeks remaining before the *Fantasia* premiere, and there was no animation camera that could move slowly and continuously enough to make that shot. But Walt wanted it.

In *Disney Animation: The Illusion of Life*, Disney animators Frank Thomas and Ollie Johnston told how Walt got it. "A couple of cameramen, two or three carpenters, two inventors, and an artist" tackled the project, wrote Thomas and Johnston.

"Walt had the carpenters knock the seats out of the end of the sound stage [which was at least forty-five feet across], shut down the recording sessions, and he told them to go ahead!"

They built a horizontal camera crane that would photograph artwork painted on panes of glass three or four feet wide. The camera was placed on a carriage that could be moved along a track. The panes of glass were mounted on movable stands so that they could be shifted out of the way as the camera moved "through" the paintings of the forest, "through" the paintings of the window-shaped light, and on to the painting of the sunburst beyond. The cameramen were quickly calibrating the camera moves in order to control the real light and do away with the reflections on the glass.

They shot day and night for six days and six nights, and the carpenters, the inventors, and the artist stood by, because they had designed and built the contraption, and if anything went wrong, they could probably fix it quickest; "the only time they had a break," wrote Thomas and Johnston, "was the one night of the week Walt played badminton on the stage from seven to ten in the evening."

When the crew finished the job, they fell into bed exhausted and rested while the film was being processed at the lab. Next day, they all looked at the exposed scene. The scene was beautiful—it didn't jerk or wobble a bit. And the scene was unusable—the wrong lens had been in the camera. In addition to the beautiful artwork, the camera had photographed the camera track, the stands that held the artwork, and even some of the workers.

"It had to be done over," wrote Thomas and Johnston. "The deadline was now only days away, but this was not the deadline for camera work, or for the lab, or for the answer print. This was the premiere showing of the picture in New York! No picture had ever been premiered with the last two hundred feet missing. The filming had to be perfect this time. The crew shot for three days and nights, stopping for a brief rest during the badminton games—then back to the figures on the floor and the careful moves. All was going well, coffee was keeping the crew awake, and a quiet determination had settled over the whole process. . . ."

And then came an earthquake. The line of wooden stands holding the glass panes rocked—but the glass painted with *Fantasia*'s final scenes did not break or even crack. When the tremor was over and another did not follow, the crew checked its equipment. It all seemed okay, but if it wasn't—if the track wasn't straight—if anything had changed, and they went ahead and finished the scene, and it turned out to jump or jerk, the ending of *Fantasia* would be ruined, and now there would be no time to reshoot it before the premiere.

The next morning, they started all over again. This time Disney canceled his badminton and barred everyone but that crew from the sound stage. They rolled the camera back to "start," put in new film—and double-checked to make sure that this time they had the right lens.

They finished shooting with one day to spare. The film was rushed off to the process lab: it was perfect.

The day of *Fantasia*'s premiere, the crew that shot the final scene took a week's vacation, and somebody else sped the end of *Fantasia* to the airport. At the airport, a motorcycle roared up. Before he had flown to New York for the premiere, Disney had given last-minute instructions for some important changes on the sound track. At the other side of the continent, the end of his picture and the entire last reel of his sound track were being put aboard the same plane!

Walt Disney was always willing to be lucky. The airplane was not grounded; it did not crash; it landed in New York with four hours to spare before the premiere. As soon as the film arrived at the Broadway Theater, it was spliced onto the end of the picture. If this had been the conventional composite of sound and picture, the sound could not have been cut in without destroying its balance. The track for Fantasound was separate, however; so the eleventh-hour addition worked just fine.

The way that Fantasound sounded was soon to be a legend. War shortages quickly made it impossible to obtain the equipment needed for further installations, and *Fantasia* with stereophonic sound had to be abandoned completely in 1941. Before that happened, however, at least one seven-year-old child begged his father to drive his mother and him the ninety-three miles from their home in rural Illinois to the Wilson Theater in Chicago—a legitimate theater wired for Fantasound—so that they could hear *Fantasia* the way that Walt Disney had intended it to be heard.

The church bells whose pure sound reached the devil at the top of Bald Mountain sounded at the rear of the theater so realistically that the child turned around in his seat. All he saw was the rest of the audience turning around to stare at the theater's rear wall. And then, his seven-year-old ears were dazzled as the sound of the *Ave Maria* chorus started at the rear of the theater and slowly and powerfully advanced to the screen speakers to join the solo voice. It was as if the spirits of the pilgrim choristers were in procession up the side aisles of the theater. Chills went up his spine—an experience that was repeated in 1982 when he went to the premiere of the forty-two-year-old *Fantasia* with its new, digitally rerecorded Dolby stereophonic sound track, at the theater of the Academy of Motion Picture Arts and Sciences in Beverly Hills. Now Irwin Kostal was conducting the Stokowski arrangements—and again he felt himself in the midst of a pilgrim chorus. It was the effect that Disney had been striving for at that December, 1938, meeting on the *Ave Maria,* when he told his story staff:

"Of course, we're taking a chance with this, but I don't feel scared about it. We've tied seven or eight shorts together and it's too much, we know that. And this [*Ave Maria*] definitely has an effect—you can't definitely tell until you've put it in there, but I think it has the right effect.

"I feel in *Snow White* we should have had something like this, something a little slower. I knew they kept cutting that prayer of Snow White's, and I would like to have been slower with that, but there was that pressure everywhere—'You've got to keep moving.' And then when we came to the coffin scene, I would like to have run that a little longer. People like those things.

"Before we finished *Snow White,* I was talking to Charlie Chaplin about it, and he said, 'Don't be afraid to let your audience wait for a few things in the picture—don't be afraid to let your tempo go slow here and there.' Well, I thought he did it too much, because I used to get itchy from watching his pictures. But it's the truth—they appreciate things more when you don't fire them too fast."

The conversation moved on to other things, but then Walt came back to tempo, saying:

"Excuse me if I get a little riled up on this stuff, because it's a continual fight around this place to get away from slapping somebody on the fanny or having somebody swallow something. So whenever it comes up I'm a little bit—I'm ready.

"It's going to take time to get ourselves up to the point where we can really get some humor in our stuff, rather than just belly laughs; and get the beauty in it, rather than just a flashy postcard. It takes time to do that, but I think we will."

Before they were through, Walt Disney, Leopold Stokowski, and their coworkers had created an entire animated concert, called *Fantasia,* to take full advantage of the animation medium. On its release in 1940, at the beginning of World War II and at least a decade before film was widely recognized as an art form worth preserving, it might have seemed vainglorious to many when Disney told *Time* magazine that he expected *Fantasia* to run for years—"perhaps even after I am gone."

Disney is gone now, but *Fantasia,* his "most exciting adventure," seems more gloriously alive with each passing year.

*What was realized of Nielsen's designs on the screen is indicated by these two frames. As the Ave Maria chorus swells to its conclusion, the predawn sky is filled with color by the coming sunrise. In the final analysis, the film was Walt Disney's Fantasia; as always, he orchestrated the work of many artists and musicians to support his philosophy of hope.*

# PRODUCTION CREDITS

## TOCCATA AND FUGUE

| | |
|---|---|
| *Direction* | Samuel Armstrong |
| *Story Development* | Lee Blair |
| | Elmer Plummer |
| | Phil Dike |
| *Art Direction* | Robert Cormack |
| *Background Paintings* | Joe Stahley |
| | John Hench |
| | Nino Carbe |
| *Animation* | Cy Young |
| | Art Palmer |
| | Daniel MacManus |
| | George Rowley |
| | Edwin Aardal |
| | Joshua Meador |
| | Cornett Wood |

## THE NUTCRACKER SUITE

| | |
|---|---|
| *Direction* | Samuel Armstrong |
| *Story Development* | Sylvia Moberly-Holland |
| | Norman Wright |
| | Albert Heath |
| | Bianca Majolie |
| | Graham Heid |
| *Character Designs* | John Walbridge |
| | Elmer Plummer |
| | Ethel Kulsar |
| *Art Direction* | Robert Cormack |
| | Al Zinnen |
| | Curtiss D. Perkins |
| | Arthur Byram |
| | Bruce Bushman |
| *Background Paintings* | John Hench |
| | Ethel Kulsar |
| | Nino Carbe |
| *Animation* | Art Babbitt |
| | Les Clark |
| | Don Lusk |
| | Cy Young |
| | Robert Stokes |

# THE SORCERER'S APPRENTICE

| | |
|---|---|
| *Direction* | James Algar |
| *Story Development* | Perce Pearce |
| | Carl Fallberg |
| *Art Direction* | Tom Codrick |
| | Charles Philippi |
| | Zack Schwartz |
| *Background Paintings* | Claude Coats |
| | Stan Spohn |
| | Albert Dempster |
| | Eric Hansen |
| *Animation Supervision* | Fred Moore |
| | Vladimir Tytla |
| *Animation* | Les Clark |
| | Riley Thomson |
| | Marvin Woodward |
| | Preston Blair |
| | Edward Love |
| | Ugo D'Orsi |
| | George Rowley |
| | Cornett Wood |

# RITE OF SPRING

| | |
|---|---|
| *Direction* | Bill Roberts |
| | Paul Satterfield |
| *Story Development & Research* | William Martin |
| | Leo Thiele |
| | Robert Sterner |
| | John Fraser McLeish |
| *Art Direction* | McLaren Stewart |
| | Dick Kelsey |
| | John Hubley |
| *Background Paintings* | Ed Starr |
| | Brice Mack |
| | Edward Levitt |
| *Animation Supervision* | Wolfgang Reitherman |
| | Joshua Meador |
| *Animation* | Philip Duncan |
| | John McManus |
| | Paul Busch |
| | Art Palmer |
| | Don Tobin |
| | Edwin Aardal |
| | Paul B. Kossoff |
| *Special Camera Effects* | Gail Papineau |
| | Leonard Pickley |

# THE PASTORAL SYMPHONY

| | |
|---|---|
| *Direction* | Hamilton Luske |
| | Jim Handley |
| | Ford Beebe |
| *Story Development* | Otto Englander |
| | Webb Smith |
| | Erdman Penner |
| | Joseph Sabo |
| | Bill Peet |
| | George Stallings |
| *Character Designs* | James Bodrero |
| | John P. Miller |
| | Lorna S. Soderstrom |
| *Art Direction* | Hugh Hennesy |
| | Kenneth Anderson |
| | J. Gordon Legg |
| | Herbert Ryman |
| | Yale Gracey |
| | Lance Nolley |
| *Background Paintings* | Claude Coats |
| | Ray Huffine |
| | W. Richard Anthony |
| | Arthur Riley |
| | Gerald Nevius |
| | Roy Forkum |
| *Animation Supervision* | Fred Moore |
| | Ward Kimball |
| | Eric Larson |
| | Art Babbitt |
| | Oliver M. Johnston, Jr. |
| | Don Towsley |
| *Animation* | Berny Wolf |
| | Jack Campbell |
| | Jack Bradbury |
| | James Moore |
| | Milt Neil |
| | Bill Justice |
| | John Elliotte |
| | Walt Kelly |
| | Don Lusk |
| | Lynn Karp |
| | Murray McClellan |
| | Robert W. Youngquist |
| | Harry Hamsel |

# DANCE OF THE HOURS

| | |
|---|---|
| *Direction* | T. Hee |
| | Norm Ferguson |
| *Character Designs* | Martin Provensen |
| | James Bodrero |
| | Duke Russell |
| | Earl Hurd |
| *Art Direction* | Kendall O'Connor |
| | Harold Doughty |
| | Ernest Nordli |
| *Background Paintings* | Albert Dempster |
| | Charles Conner |
| *Animation Supervision* | Norm Ferguson |
| *Animation* | John Lounsbery |
| | Howard Swift |
| | Preston Blair |
| | Hugh Fraser |
| | Harvey Toombs |
| | Norman Tate |
| | Hicks Lokey |
| | Art Elliott |
| | Grant Simmons |
| | Ray Patterson |
| | Franklin Grundeen |

# NIGHT ON BALD MOUNTAIN/AVE MARIA

| | |
|---|---|
| *Direction* | Wilfred Jackson |
| *Story Development* | Campbell Grant |
| | Arthur Heinemann |
| | Phil Dike |
| *Art Direction* | Kay Nielsen |
| | Terrell Stapp |
| | Charles Payzant |
| | Thor Putnam |
| *Background Paintings* | Merle Cox |
| | Ray Lockrem |
| | Robert Storms |
| | W. Richard Anthony |
| *Animation Supervision* | Vladimir Tytla |
| *Animation* | John McManus |
| | William N. Shull |
| | Robert W. Carlson, Jr. |
| | Lester Novros |
| | Don Patterson |
| *Special Animation Effects* | Joshua Meador |
| | Miles E. Pike |
| | John F. Reed |
| | Daniel MacManus |
| *Special Camera Effects* | Gail Papineau |
| | Leonard Pickley |
| *Ave Maria Chorus* | Charles Henderson, Director |
| | Julietta Novis, Soloist |

# FOR ALL SEQUENCES

| | |
|---|---|
| *Production Supervision* | Ben Sharpsteen |
| *Story Direction* | Joe Grant |
| | Dick Huemer |
| *Musical Direction* | Edward H. Plumb |
| *Musical Film Editor* | Stephen Csillag |
| *Recording* | William E. Garity |
| | C. O. Slyfield |
| | J. N. A. Hawkins |

My primary sources for the writing of this book were the *Fantasia* files in the Disney Archives — particularly the stenographic notes on Walt Disney's story conferences when he was planning the film — and my own interviews with people who worked on *Fantasia*, starting with Disney himself. In addition, however, many books and articles helped me piece together the story of the production, and understand the techniques involved, and the most important of those are listed here.

## BOOKS

CHARLOT, JEAN. *Art from the Mayans to Disney.* New York: Sheed and Ward, 1939.

CULHANE, JOHN. *Retrospectives: Walt Disney.* Zagreb, Yugoslavia: Zagreb Film, 1974.

————. *Special Effects in the Movies.* New York: Ballantine Books, 1981.

EISENSTEIN, SERGEI. *Film Essays and a Lecture.* Ed. Jay Leyda. New York: Praeger, 1970.

————. *The Film Sense.* New York: Harcourt, Brace & Co., 1942.

FEILD, R. D. *The Art of Walt Disney.* New York: Macmillan, 1942.

FERGUSON, OTIS. *The Film Criticism of Otis Ferguson.* Philadelphia: Temple University Press, 1971.

FINCH, CHRISTOPHER. *The Art of Walt Disney: From Mickey Mouse to the Magic Kingdoms.* New York: Harry N. Abrams, 1973.

————. *Walt Disney's America.* New York: Abbeville Press, 1978.

GOMBRICH, E. H. *Art and Illusion.* Princeton, N.J.: Princeton University Press, 1960.

GOULD, STEPHEN JAY. *Ever Since Darwin: Reflections in Natural History.* New York: W. W. Norton & Co., 1977.

GRAHAM, DONALD W. *Composing Pictures.* New York: Van Nostrand Reinhold Co., 1970.

JACOBS, LEWIS. *The Emergence of Film Art.* New York: Hopkinson and Blake, 1969.

————. *Rise of the American Film.* New York: Harcourt Brace, 1939.

MILLER, DIANE DISNEY (as told to Pete Martin). *The Story of Walt Disney.* New York: Holt, 1957.

READ, HERBERT. *Art and Alienation.* New York: Horizon Press, 1967.

SCHICKEL, RICHARD. *The Disney Version.* New York: Simon & Schuster, 1968.

STOKOWSKI, LEOPOLD. *Music for All of Us.* New York: Simon & Schuster, 1943.

STRAVINSKY, IGOR, and ROBERT CRAFT. *Expositions and Developments.* New York: Doubleday, 1962.

STRAVINSKY, VERA, and ROBERT CRAFT. *Stravinsky in Pictures and Documents.* New York: Simon & Schuster, 1979.

TALBOT, DANIEL. *Film: An Anthology.* New York: Simon & Schuster, 1959. Includes Irwin Panofsky's essay "Style and Medium in the Motion Pictures" (1934), with an updated note on *Fantasia.*

TAYLOR, DEEMS. *Walt Disney's Fantasia.* New York: Simon & Schuster, 1940.

THOMAS, BOB. *Walt Disney: An American Original.* New York: Simon & Schuster, 1976.

————. *Walt Disney: The Art of Animation.* New York: Golden Press, 1958.

THOMAS, FRANK, and OLLIE JOHNSTON. *Disney Animation: The Illusion of Life.* New York: Abbeville Press, 1981.

WALT DISNEY PRODUCTIONS. *Ave Maria, an Interpretation from Walt Disney's Fantasia.* Inspired by the music of Franz Schubert; lyrics by Rachel Field. New York: Random House, 1940.

————. *Dance of the Hours, from Walt Disney's Fantasia.* New York: Harper, 1940.

————. *The Nutcracker Suite, from Walt Disney's Fantasia.* Introduction by Leopold Stokowski, with Six Special Arrangements for Piano by Frederick Stark. Boston: Little, Brown and Co., 1940.

————. *Pastoral, from Walt Disney's Fantasia.* New York: Harper, 1940.

————. *The Sorcerer's Apprentice, from Walt Disney's Fantasia.* New York: Grosset and Dunlap, 1940.

————. *Stories from Walt Disney's Fantasia.* New York: Random House, 1940.

ARTICLES

BELMONT, I. J. "Painter of Music Criticizes 'Fantasia.' " *Art Digest,* December 15, 1940.

BLAIR, PRESTON. "The Animation of 'Fantasia.' " *Cartoonist Profiles,* March 1981.

BLAKE, LARRY. "Re-Recording and Post-Production for Disney's Fantasia." *Recording Engineer/Producer,* October 1982.

BOONE, ANDREW R. "Mickey Mouse Goes Classical." *Popular Science Monthly,* January 1941.

BOSWELL, PEYTON. "The Wonder of Fantasia." *Art Digest,* December 1, 1940.

BRYAN, JAMES A. "The Inside Dope on Fantasia." *Coast FM and Fine Arts,* April 1970.

CHASINS, ABRAM. "Stokowski's Legend—Mickey Mouse to Mahler." *New York Times,* April 18, 1982.

CULHANE, JOHN. "The Last of the Nine Old Men." *American Film,* June 1977.

————. "The Old Disney Magic." *New York Times Magazine,* August 1, 1976.

————. "Tripping on *Fantasia.*" *Newsweek,* January 19, 1970.

"Disney's Cinesymphony." *Time,* November 18, 1940.

DOWNES, OLIN. "Disney's Experiment: Second Thoughts on 'Fantasia' and Its Visualization of Music." *New York Times,* November 17, 1940.

FANTEL, HANS. "Stokowski, an Audio Prophet." *New York Times,* May 30, 1982.

GARITY, WILLIAM E., and J. N. A. HAWKINS. "Fantasound." *Journal of the Society of Motion Picture Engineers,* August 1941.

GARITY, WILLIAM E., and WATSON JONES. "Experiences in Road-showing Walt Disney's Fantasia." *Journal of the Society of Motion Picture Engineers,* July 1942.

HOLLISTER, PAUL. "Walt Disney: Genius at Work." *Atlantic Monthly,* December 1940.

ISAACS, HERMINE RICH. "New Horizons: Fantasia and Fantasound." *Theatre Arts,* January 1941.

LEWIN, FRANK. "Fantasia Revisited." *Film Music,* January-February 1956.

LORENTZ, PARE. Review of *Fantasia. McCalls,* February 1941.

LOW, DAVID. "Leonardo da Disney." *The New Republic,* January 5, 1942.

MORITZ, WILLIAM. "The Films of Oskar Fischinger." *Film Culture,* Nos. 58-60, 1974.

NEWSOM, JON. " 'A Sound Idea'/Music for Animated Films." *The Film Quarterly Journal of the Library of Congress,* Summer-Fall 1980.

———. "Igor Stravinsky: 1882-1971." *Saturday Review,* May 29, 1971. An entire issue devoted to the composer, which contains Deems Taylor's initial reaction to Stravinsky's *Rite of Spring* in *Fantasia.*

PECK, A. P. "What Makes 'Fantasia' Click." *Scientific American,* January 1941.

PLUMB, EDWARD H. "The Future of Fantasound." *Journal of the Society of Motion Picture Engineers,* July 1942.

SMITH, DAVID R. *"The Sorcerer's Apprentice:* Birthplace of *Fantasia." Millimeter,* February 1976.

THOMPSON, VIRGIL. Review of *Fantasia* (musical point of view). *New York Herald Tribune,* November 14, 1940.

WALT DISNEY PRODUCTIONS. *"bulletin: 'FANTASIA' Edition,"* November 15, 1940. The issue of the Studio house organ devoted to the production of *Fantasia.*

———. *An Introduction to the Walt Disney Studios.* 1938. A booklet giving a brief outline of the Studio's principal departments and an explanation to artists of its employment policies as *Fantasia* went into production.

———. *Walt Disney Presents FANTASIA.* 1940. Souvenir program for the premiere engagement.

———. *Walt Disney Presents FANTASIA in Stereophonic Sound.* 1977. Souvenir program for the 1977 re-release of *Fantasia.*

WASSERMAN, NORMAN. "Special Projection Process Gives 'Fantasia' New Look." *International Projectionist,* March 1956.

# ACKNOWLEDGMENTS

Walt Disney's daughter, Diane, now Mrs. Ron Miller, wife of the president of Walt Disney Productions, arranged for me to meet her father when I was seventeen. We talked a lot about *Fantasia* in his super-duper backyard that Sunday afternoon in August of 1951, and Walt invited me to visit his Studio the following Wednesday, where he arranged for me to meet two artists who had worked on *Fantasia,* Les Clark and Ward Kimball. So my thanks go first of all to Diane, and to the officers of Walt Disney Productions—Ron Miller, Card Walker, Vince Jefferds, Thomas L. Wilhite—who have made me feel as welcome at that studio for thirty-one years as I felt the day I first walked, at Walt's invitation, up Mickey Mouse Boulevard.

In particular, I am grateful to Vince Jefferds, Senior Vice-President, Walt Disney Marketing Division. Vince went out of his way to make sure that I had continuing access to all the stenographic notes taken at *Fantasia* story meetings, so that this book could accurately present the role that Walt himself played in the making of *Fantasia.* Everyone in Vince's department did what they could to help me, so thanks also to Wendall Mohler, Don McLaughlin, Wayne Morris, and Pat Lawson.

All who write about Walt Disney and his Studio know that the Disney Archives constitute the best research facility on those subjects in the world, thanks to many years of patient and painstaking research into all aspects of the Studio's history by David R. Smith, Disney archivist. Stokowski's letter describing his first meeting with Walt is found there; the photograph of Disney and Stravinsky that Stravinsky autographed to Walt is on the wall; articles on and reviews of the films are gathered in scrapbooks; taped interviews with those who made the Studio's history are transcribed and indexed. In addition to being the most knowledgeable guide to all these treasures, David has written the most reliable article on *Fantasia* (included in this book's bibliography). And he and his assistants, Paula Sigman and Rose Motzko, are indefatigable in checking names and dates and spellings and titles and locations.

The Disney Studio has also saved nearly every piece of art produced in connection with its pictures, and those that appear in this book were located for me by the Animation Research Team under LeRoy Anderson. When I have written about *Fantasia* over the years for *Newsweek,* the *New York Times Magazine, Reader's Digest,* and *American Film,* help has come from Walt's brother, Roy Disney, and from Irving Ludwig, Mal Barbour, and Tom Jones.

At Harry N. Abrams, I was delighted to have as my editor Darlene Geis, a longtime *Fantasia* fan who is enthusiastic about art and music and writing. Her sensitive contributions were greatly appreciated. Our happy collaboration began the day that she and I and Sam Antupit, director of art and design at Abrams and this book's designer, watched *Fantasia* again at a private screening arranged by Erwin D. Okun and Bob King of the Disney staff. I learned that *Fantasia* in its world premiere engagement was the first film that Darlene and her husband saw when they moved to New York. Then one day at the Abrams offices I chanced upon a "Guess the Employees from Their Baby Pictures" contest on the design department's bulletin board and correctly guessed that the tyke holding the stuffed Mickey Mouse was young Sam. This was my cue to bring out the book my parents gave me for Christmas when I was six: *Stories from Walt Disney's Fantasia.*

Knowing that I used the *Pastoral Symphony* story as a primer ("Baby Pegasus was a little horse with wings," it began), you can imagine the pleasure I have had tracking down artists who worked on *Fantasia* to learn the story of its production. At the First World Retrospective of Animation Cinema, held in conjunction with Expo '67 in Montreal, Art Babbitt and Bill Tytla were my guides. When I was cohost of the Walt Disney Productions 50th Anniversary Retrospective at New York's Lincoln Center in 1973, I talked *Fantasia* with Jim Algar, director of *The Sorcerer's Apprentice,* and Ken Anderson, an art director of *The Pastoral Symphony.* As master of ceremonies of Disney on Film: A Forum on Animation and Fantasy Film-Making in the 80's, I toured American colleges and universities in 1981 with Wolfgang "Woolie" Reitherman, who animated the climactic dinosaur fight in *Rite of Spring,* and Eric Larson, who made Baby Pegasus fly. Then there were the evenings I spent at the homes of Dick Huemer, one of *Fantasia*'s two story directors; John Hubley, an art director of *Rite of Spring* (who gave me his personal copy of the *Fantasia* edition of *the bulletin,* the Disney Studio employees' newspaper); and Ollie Johnston, animator on *The Pastoral Symphony.* There were memorable lunches, dinners, meetings, or viewings of the film with *Fantasia* artists Aurelius Battaglia, Al Dempster, Jules Engel, T. Hee, John Hench, Bill Hurtz, Wilfred Jackson, John Lounsbery, Daniel MacManus, Reg Massie, Grim Natwick, Don Patterson, Ray Patterson, George Rowley, Art Scott, and Norman Tate. And there are eight animation artists who did not work on *Fantasia* but who elucidated for me the work of those who did: Milt Kahl, Marc Davis, Frank Thomas, Bob Clampett, Chuck Jones, Ray Favata, George Bakes, and Shamus Culhane. My fervent thanks to them all.

Above all, it is my wife, Hind, who has made this project such an enjoyable experience. Her love of music and the graphic arts is so intense that I never hesitated to suggest we reexperience *Fantasia* one more time. And depending on where we were, and how old our two sons were, we saw a different film every time. Our older son, Michael, graduated in film from Ithaca College this year, and I can still see him as a ten-year-old the night Art Babbitt came to dinner, gravely questioning the great animator about the way he animated *Fantasia*'s mushroom dance. The younger, T.H., is a junior at Harvard now, and, I trust, is being treated understandingly by his professors: when he was two, neither dinosaurs nor the devil fazed him, but he had to be carried out of the theater in tears when the Sorcerer spanked Mickey.

It is further enjoyment to imagine that this book will remind readers where they were, when, and with whom, each time they have experienced *Fantasia*—and that the memories thus activated will make them happy.

# INDEX

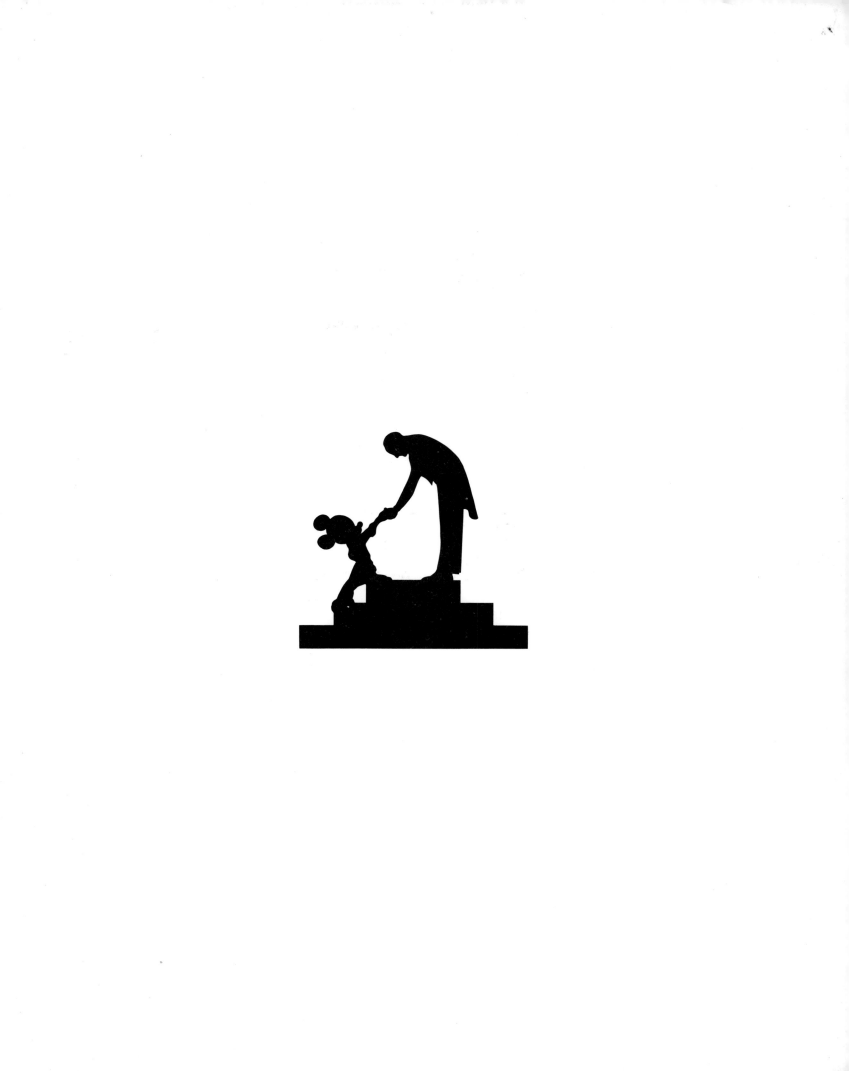

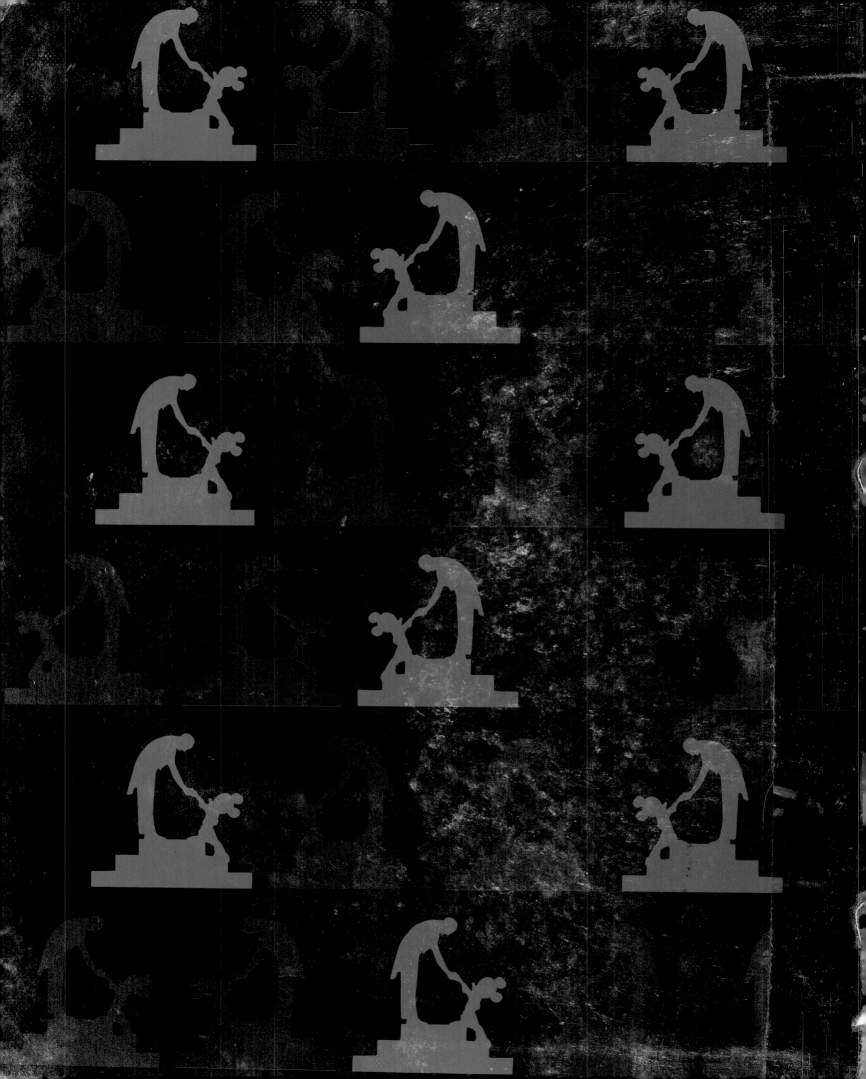